The Core Agreements

BILL WAITS

For John Waits, from whom I learned to look at the world again with a child's
eye and live every day with energy

1 WALTER'S STORY

I would like to start this book by talking about a close story. Some time ago, a middle-aged man named Walter came to my office. He seemed like a nice guy, with a smile on his face and good manners. "Doctor, I have lived the wrong life. "I don't want to continue like this," he told me when I asked him the reason for his visit to my office. I asked him for a little more information, because as is well known, a wrong life depends a lot from where you look at it. What is wrong for some may be very right for others. Then he began his story.

When he was fifteen years old, Walter believed that people were just another instrument in life. He thought of his environment as a tool to reach his goal. As he explained to me, he was fully aware that it was a petty idea, but he said that at his young age he was already disappointed in the world enough to lose faith in humanity. "Doctor, I couldn't stand the eternal discourse about the fraternization of humans. I knew the origin of that word with its French root frère, which translates as brother. But what the hell were they talking about if the history of the Judeo-Catholic tradition and all Western religions is based on a savage fratricide like that of Cain in against Abel?" His story was undoubtedly captivating. He had the ability to speak without fear about ideas of which he was not very proud.

As he told me, he was aware of the ignoble nature of his ideas, but he believed that at his young age he was so disappointed in human society as to entertain this type of thoughts: "people are instruments and they only serve if they are useful for a purpose." ".

"Doctor, when I looked around I couldn't find anything other than confirmation of that idea. Everything was misery and greed, war, hunger, destruction," he said and illustrated me with examples. He spoke of the years in which the world was creaking at its foundations, civil wars were setting the Balkans on fire, the collapse of the Soviet Union was celebrated by savage neoliberalism and the news repeated over and over again that the hole in the ozone layer was growing steadily. stall.

"How could I think of anything but disappointment about our species?" Young Walter was somewhat right, but I was extremely intrigued as to how this misanthropic and mean young man had come to my office turned into what seemed like a good man.

Walter continued his story and told me the consequences of his conception of life: seeing people that way did not allow him to open up enough to be able to establish a network of friends that would make his youth a time of happiness. "I lived on the defensive. I was convinced that everyone around me had bad feelings in their hearts, hidden behind fake smiles, and I had a hard time even trusting my parents. They were not bad people, but I believed that they were at least to blame for my suffering for giving me the problem of existence. So my relationship with them was not very fluid either. I went home from school only to lock myself in my room to read comics and listen to heavy rock. He fit perfectly into what today could be considered a problem child with the potential to do something horrible like those Columbine kids did. The texts I read then were full of hatred towards the human species, so my situation was reinforced by an entire theoretical framework that gave rise to absurd feelings."

Listening to it was overwhelming. The man had great narrative abilities and in his speech you could feel the sadness for a past that was impossible to modify. The worst came later, he told me. "When I try to think about what happened, I feel like there was another person inside me." Before finishing high school, Walter began to flirt with extreme right-wing ideas and soon followed neo-Nazi ideologies. "In this group I found people who had a vision of life similar to mine. They were kids like me, disappointed in humanity, full of irrational hatred who believed that humanity was lost and that none of the values that supposedly governed our society were real."

Despite finding a social group, Walter was not happy. "It is very difficult to find happiness when you live with hate. Those kids and I were lost without knowing it. We believed ourselves to be superior to the rest of the people because we thought we had clear ideas and we doubted everything that was proposed to us. At first we met to discuss texts by some authors such as Nietzsche or Schopenhauer, but of course, we distorted their meaning to make it coincide with our values. Over time we planned some pretty deplorable activities, like writing certain slogans on city walls or harassing people in vulnerable conditions. Today I remember all this with a shame that is difficult for me to bear." At this point, Walter paused in his story and cried, hiding his face in his hands. "It was a very dark time, because at the same time I suffered a misfortune that marked my life. My parents died in a tragic road accident. I couldn't tell them that I loved them, I was so full of hatred and disappointment that at that time I thought of their death as a great relief to me. Oh my god, I was so stupid I couldn't see what was happening. The only people in the world who showed selfless love for me had just disappeared and I was relieved. But of course, time would take care of putting me in my place. I was twenty years old and had a mediocre job in a fast food chain, at night I drank alcohol in the solitude of my house and on weekends I went to the absurd meetings of my group of misfits in which we planned how to do the job. more miserable life for those who already had enough with their vulnerability. The hatred he felt for society only grew. Maybe that's why I volunteered when our group of criminals hiding behind a headless ideology decided we should beat up some black kids. We went in a group, like cowards, to the basketball court where they used to play and we chose two at random. We beat them mercilessly with baseball bats. One of them lost several teeth because of us. After a week the police came to my house. Someone had identified me and I had to answer for the attack. In state court, my supposed 'brigade' companions disappeared. Only one of them testified and accused me of being the leader of the group and of having planned everything. During the raid on my house they found Nazi literature and a long list of trash that incriminated me. At the end of the day they were right. I was not the leader of the group but I had allowed myself to be manipulated like an idiot. What's more, I had felt a certain pride in being able to carry out that evil. I was sentenced to three years in prison, reviewable after eighteen months. He was twenty-one years old and his life was destroyed. Prison was a hell I couldn't describe. It only increased my hatred for society and the system. It all seemed to me like a crude play designed to make humans believe that their lives had some meaning. By then, I knew very well the resource of complaint and I was an expert in the art of meaningless lamentation, because in some way I knew that adopting the role of victim allowed me to escape from my responsibilities. The concept of prison rehabilitation does not make much sense. There people cook in their own hatred. That happened to me during my stay. I didn't understand that the fault for what had happened to me was mine alone. I considered myself a victim of the hypocrisy of the system. I tried to seek refuge in reading, but the prison texts seemed empty, meaningless. Many of them were linked to religion and spoke to me about values that I could not find anywhere. At some point I thought that perhaps the best thing for my spirit would be suicide. Leaving this world forever, because nothing made sense."

"I left there without experiencing any rehabilitation. It is true that my reflections took me away from the absurd world of white supremacy, but I still believed that people were just tools to achieve an end. Of course, I didn't know what that goal was in my life. I found a mediocre job and my routine was very similar to the one I had before entering prison: I would go from my house to my job and return with a broken body to sit in front of the television with a beer in my hand. Beer after beer lulled me into unconsciousness. The next day I woke up with a hellish headache that only a beer for breakfast could calm. The wheel turned again and the routine was repeated. Three years passed in a similar situation. I felt pain in different parts of my body, but nothing seemed to bother me enough to change my habits. By then I was no longer thinking about people, I was no longer thinking about society, I was no longer thinking about anything other than my check at the end of the month to make sure I could finance my beers and junk food that filled my afternoons. I gained weight and changed my appearance. He was not yet thirty years old and already seemed aged, defeated. Living in bitterness has its price. I knew it when one afternoon in front of the dishwasher I felt a sharp pain in the small of my back. It was a raw pain, as if I had been pierced with a burning rod. I had never felt something like this before: in my absurd time in the supremacist brigades I received more than one blow, but this was different. My body was creaking inside and the pain was so unbearable that I passed out. When I regained consciousness, I crawled as best I could to the door of my apartment to ask for help. A man called 911 and an ambulance showed up shortly to take me to the hospital. The paramedics analyzed me on the way and commented things to each other that I couldn't understand. They injected me with a powerful painkiller that made me go into a state of disconnection until the next day. When I opened my eyes, more than twelve hours had passed since I was admitted to the hospital. He was wearing a white coat and had an IV attached to his arm. Shortly after, a nurse appeared there and greeted me with a friendly gesture. 'You were lucky, if it weren't for your neighbor I would have died at home,' he told me and explained that the help I received saved my life. I suffered internal bleeding and during the examination the doctors found that my kidneys were destroyed. A doctor confirmed the diagnosis: I would need a transplant urgently. If he didn't find a donor, he would be dead in a few months. The news hit me like a bucket of cold water. Fate seemed to take revenge on me with a dirty trick. Now it would depend on humanity if it wanted to remain among the living. I entered the national waiting list but it was not a priority: there were a large number of people in front of me, so much so that I could not wait for the public system to find a kidney for my body. I left the hospital with a small machine that I had to connect to every night for dialysis, but this would not be enough for a while. Would this be the end of me? I asked myself constantly. Had my life been of any use? The deep feeling of having let the days go by wrapped in hatred only increased my hatred of the world. At that moment I couldn't understand that all the problems I had gone through throughout my life were my fault. "I considered myself a victim of circumstances and I was convinced that all the tragedies I had experienced proved me right."

"Stunned by the prospect of death, I left my job and locked myself in my home, willing to sit and wait with a beer in my hand. I spent weeks like this, despite doctors' recommendations. I did my dialysis at night, after drinking beer and watching television. It's hard for me to remember those days clearly. I don't know if it's due to excess alcohol or the feeling of hopelessness, but today it all seems like part of a nightmare experienced by someone else. Just when I thought my death was around the corner, the doorbell to my apartment rang. I didn't feel like seeing anyone and I let it be. But the person on the other side insisted. The sound interrupted the TV, so I got up and opened it. I met the face of my neighbor, the black man who had called 911 when I suffered my hemorrhage. He introduced himself with a smile: 'My name is Tim, I wanted to know how you were doing and if you would like to spend Thanksgiving with my family,' he said, extending his hand towards me. I stared at him and closed the door in his face, without answering a single word. What did this man think he came to seek my friendship? After a few minutes , the doorbell rang again insistently. If I wanted to listen to the television I had to open that door and get rid of that man, so I got up in a bad mood, ready to unleash a long list of insults. I opened it suddenly and was greatly surprised when I found a black girl, probably Tim's daughter, who was holding a card in her hands. The little girl must have been about seven years old and had two braids in her hair. His teeth were white as milk and his eyes had the shine of ten thousand diamonds. 'My daddy says you need love. 'I made you this card,' she told me and held it out to me before running away embarrassed. I returned to my couch and my beer with the card in my hand. It was a school cardboard folded in half. It had a drawing of a poorly outlined heart and a white man with a glass in his hand. With childish handwriting he said: "I hope you get better soon." It had been almost ten years since my parents died and many more since the last time someone said a thing like that to me. I couldn't help but think nostalgically about the passage of time and the roller coaster that my life had been until then. A rebellious tear appeared on my face despite all the times I declared myself a man who never intended to cry. I felt a little ashamed of the feelings that card gave me. The whole situation was absurd. Why did this girl and her father appear before me to ruin my life? What could change at this point, when everything seemed written? I took the card in my hand, crumpled it and threw it away, as if the gesture would allow me to expel all human beings from the face of the earth.

"The next day I woke up with my usual hangover. My head was like a big pressure cooker ready to explode so I took two aspirin. My refrigerator was empty: without food or beer, I had to go out to that inhospitable land that for me was the street. I took the opportunity to pick up the discarded cans and containers of frozen pizza that littered my living room, put everything in a large garbage bag and headed towards the street. At the dumpster I met Tim. 'Good morning, Walter. How are things going for you on this beautiful day?' His greeting seemed absurd to me. One day after closing the door in his face, that man still wanted to talk. 'Fine,' I just answered and got out of there as soon as I could. 'I'm very happy, I see that today you want to talk more. I live with my family in apartment 202,' Tim said as I walked away from him. Why are there people who want to give without receiving? What was behind that kindness? Surely there would be something, because no one gives anything without expecting something. Those were some of the reflections I had on my way to the supermarket. Also, how the hell did he know my name? It was clear that this man wanted something and his attitude had given him away. I made my purchases with that idea burning in my heart. But this would not stay like this. When I got back, that guy Tim was going to listen to me. Yes sir. After leaving the shopping bags, I went out ready to face that man. Department 202, he said, that's where he would go. I rang her bell and in a few seconds the girl who had offered me the card appeared at the door. A sweet aroma of cinnamon filled the atmosphere and the little girl's smile greeted me: 'Ah, it's you. It's good that you've come! My daddy is waiting for him,' he turned around and shouted: 'daddy, the neighbor who needs our love is here.' His honesty made me smile. I imagined the family gathered at dinner and Tim saying, 'Well, we have to give our love to the poor guy from 101. He needs love.' The situation seemed absurd and somehow abhorrent to me. I didn't want anyone's pity. I didn't need it. I had survived without indulgences and I could continue doing so until my kidneys said enough. Tim appeared with his daughter in his arms. The girl's smile was contagious and when she saw me again in her doorway she insisted to her father: 'here is the man who needs love.' He told her that we all need love and that I was no exception. 'Don't you think you need love too?' Tim asked the little girl. The scene disarmed me. Part of the anger that I brought with me fell to the floor like a heavy bag of dirty clothes and I only managed to ask the little girl 'What is your name?'. 'Laetitia, but they call me La. You can tell me La'. His father smiled kindly at me and asked me what brought me to him. 'Have you changed your mind about Thanksgiving dinner?' I shook my head in the negative and tried to get back to my thoughts. 'Listen, I don't know what you're up to, but you better not continue with this. I don't know what you want from me, but you're not going to get very far.' His face contorted, surprised. 'Listen, Walter, I don't know what you think, but I have something to suggest to you. Come and have a coffee with us, Trishia is baking some cookies that wouldn't hurt to share,' as she said this she touched her belly as a sign of fatness and little La imitated it. The smell was irresistible, but a voice inside me told me that accepting anything from that man would be betraying my entire past. 'Don't waste your time on me,' I said and turned around. Back in my apartment, an idea ran through my mind: Why should I accept the friendship of a stranger? Why does a black man want to be my friend if it's obvious that's who I am? The cloudy lullaby of alcohol enveloped me once again until I lost consciousness.

"Two days later I woke up drenched in sweat due to a pain similar to the stab that took me to the hospital. As the pain increased, I became convinced that I wouldn't make it this time. I staggered to the entrance of my apartment, opened the door and collapsed like the first time. What happened next is a haze: sirens, screams, dreams, tunnels, emptiness, doctors, blood, artificial respirators, volcanic landscapes, deep blue, my childhood memory, me as a child playing with a baseball, my mother's smile and total darkness. I opened my eyes and the sound of my heart rate monitor gave me an idea of where I was. It took me a few minutes to sit up. I had a feeling of heaviness and pain throughout my abdomen. I tried to sit up on the hospital bed, but a tight bandage around my torso prevented me from doing so. I let my head fall back onto the pillow and looked around. I was in a shared pavilion and my space was delimited by a curtain. After a few minutes, a nurse opened the curtain and was surprised to see me conscious. 'Oh, wow, I see you're back with us.' Everything seemed strange around me, except for the man lying in the bed next to me: his face was familiar to me, but my brain was moving very slowly. It was Tim. Why the hell was my apartment neighbor next to me? For a moment I feared I had done something wrong during the alcohol unconsciousness. Tim watched me from his bed as he ate what looked like a flan. 'Wow, you're finally back! We thought we wouldn't have you for dinner,' he said with a laugh and added, 'after all, it looks like we'll be celebrating Thanksgiving together after all, Walter.' The nurse returned accompanied by a doctor. They examined me gently and the doctor said, 'Well, things seem to be progressing positively. I think you owe this man a hug, he saved his life,' he said, pointing to Tim. How could I understand all that? 'I think you haven't understood. This man donated one of his kidneys to her. We performed the emergency operation and everything indicates that his recovery is progressing well. In a few weeks you will be almost as good as new,' the doctor joked."

"The news was an atomic bomb in my spirit. How could it be possible that a guy I barely knew had sacrificed years of his life to prolong mine? I couldn't understand anything that was happening, everything seemed like a macabre joke of fate, it wasn't possible that after all life would give me a new opportunity in the hands of that man, a guy whom I had absurdly prejudiced because of his race and whom he had despised. 'And who authorized them to give me their kidney!?' I asked the doctor with burning hatred. 'Why didn't anyone ask me if I wanted his kidney?' I insisted. 'You did it yourself. During his first admission to the hospital he filled out a series of documents that authorized us to act in case he was unconscious and that is precisely what we did,' the doctor answered me, visibly upset. 'Instead of asking those kinds of stupid questions you should be thanking this man and fate for the opportunity they give you. Do you think everyone has their luck?' The doctor left the ward and I fell silent, lulled by the sound of the vital signs monitor and the back and forth of my thoughts. Tim looked at me seriously and after a while said:

'Hey, brother, I don't want your thanks, but at least I think I deserve some of your dinner' and pointed with his lips to a tray of food arranged next to my bed. . It was incredible. The man had given me a kidney that I refused to accept and yet he maintained his appetite and good humor. I took a deep breath and sat up on the stretcher as best I could to reach the tray. With difficulty I dragged her towards her bed and said a word I had rarely uttered in my life: 'Thank you.' The sound of these letters was like a sacred mantra that was hidden inside me and with which something was unlocked in my soul. Tim looked at me with a curious gesture that I understood as 'don't worry, man, that's what we're here for', but I was worried. He and I had barely exchanged a few words and they weren't exactly the kindest of me, but even so he had me given the most precious gift a man could ever receive. For the first time in my adult life, I burst into tears. They were the tears accumulated during a life of hatred, a life dedicated to aggressiveness and contempt for others, it was crying for everything I had stopped seeing, how could I be so stupid, I told myself, if the truth was there to whoever wants to see it: good people exist and it is not necessary to look under the stones, the true parameters of life for every human being must be kindness and generosity. 'I don't deserve it, I don't deserve it,' I repeated over and over again between my tears. I truly believed that I did not deserve the blessing that human being was giving me. He seemed displeased with my words and interrupted me. 'Listen, brother, I know very well who you are and what you think. I know you more than you think. I know that you were in prison and I know very well the reasons... That's why I think you deserve a new chance. People like you are no different than people like me, or like him or her... we all need love, affection and understanding. And I'm not going to sit at home waiting for someone to offer love. I'm going to give it, because I know that this is a chain of favors.' Tim talked like a Sunday preacher while I sobbed. The other patients in the ward followed the scene with interest and an elderly man threatened to applaud his speech, but the cast on his arm prevented him from doing so.

"The lesson was clear: being a good person will make others good people. Tim taught me a lot more than he thought and I couldn't let him down. A few months have passed since that episode and I have tried in every way to follow his example. However, sometimes hopelessness and disappointment in humanity resurfaces in my heart. That is why I have come to you, doctor: I want to talk in detail about everything I have experienced so that I can let go of this heavy burden and become a person like Tim, willing to give without waiting, knowing that each gesture of kindness will make this world a better place. better place".

Walter's story left me speechless. My consultation seemed charged with a special energy, as if an invisible connection had been established between us, an unbreakable bond between human beings represented there by two unknown men and at the same time moved by a story of transformation that was just beginning. "Walter, thank you so much for sharing this powerful story with me. Welcome, I am not the best person on Earth, but I swear that every morning I wake up with the goal of trying. I hope you try it with me," I told him and we shook hands. For him, in large part, these lessons of personal growth are dedicated, because deep down I know that he will become a vitamin person. .

2 THE PERSON YOU WOULD LIKE TO HAVE NEAR

The Argentine writer Roberto Fontanarrosa was once asked what he wanted for his son and he responded: "May his friends be happy to see him coming." This is perhaps one of the best definitions of friendship I know. It is simple and encompasses barbaric wisdom. It tells us about the depth and simplicity of human relationships and leaves us with a lesson that I would like to delve into: to be a nice person is to be the person with whom you would like to share your time. Have you ever thought about that? Why do we like to share our leisure moments with certain people? Is it just because we share similar interests like literature or Queen songs? Is it because we went to school together when we were children and we are linked by a common past that has created an indelible bond even though we think completely differently on almost all of life's fundamental issues? And, above all, the basic question: could we be our own friends?

A few years ago I began to ask myself the same thing: if I walked into a cafe and by chance bumped into myself and started a conversation, would I like him? The automatic response is usually a nervous yes. Years of guilty education have driven us towards the modesty of humility and the denial of egocentrism, generating a curious rebound effect in which we love each other without love.

When I was asked to write this book, I had a series of reflections about what I believed it was to be a "vitamin" person or a magnetic person. I looked in the rearview mirror of my life in search of all those people whom I considered excellent company and whom I wanted to have by my side. Along the way I met a series of people with very diverse and disparate personalities. I spent a long time thinking about why, despite being so different from each other, each of them had managed to make such a pleasant and lasting impression on me. I made a mental list of the qualities of each of them and after a while I concluded that they had certain similarities that I will explain throughout this book. However, one of the things that surprised me most about my account was understanding that all the magnetic people in my life had the capacity to be unique in their own way. None of them wanted to follow a pattern and they had a security of character that made them strong and admirable. In short, each one was pure and pursued his essence without wanting to fit into the crowd. It was then that the basic concept that I will work on in this text came to mind: be yourself. I will say it again, because it seems like a simple teaching, but it is essential to be free: be yourself. Don't try to be like anyone else and never let other people's opinions shape your character. The essence of magnetic people is precisely to resemble themselves solely and exclusively, even when they all share a series of values that will reinforce this magnetism.

When I was in school I met a particular girl. Their clothes seemed straight out of a 1940s movie and challenged the already bizarre fashion of the 1970s. He sat in his seat and took out a notebook, which he immersed himself in as soon as the teacher began to speak. Sometimes I lost track of the class and wanted to look over his shoulder to pick up the lesson. What I found in his notebook had absolutely nothing to do with what that biology teacher explained. It was a literary text that at that time seemed like a story to me. This girl had no friends at school and every afternoon she ate lunch alone in the cafeteria, always accompanied by a book. Among my classmates, the girl was considered a "freak" and few were interested in her life. I once wanted to break this isolation and approached her and her book during lunch. I greeted her and she responded with a sweet smile. "Have you come to make fun of me?" his question seemed honest, free of hatred. I answered no, that I was just curious about her and her eternal book. "Oh, it's not eternal, Jane Austen is with me today," she replied smiling. "You can imagine that I change books from time to time, otherwise it would be very boring to always read the same novel, don't you think?" she asked me, amused, and invited me to sit next to her. She explained to me that she didn't feel the need to belong to the group and that she never felt alone. "Literature always accompanies me, it's incredible what you can experience with a book," she told me and then asked: "Do you also think I'm a freak?" I nodded embarrassed, because that sweet girl was nicer than I thought, but I couldn't lie to her. Until that day, I thought the same as my classmates: "what a strange creature who doesn't want to be fashionable." "You don't have to be ashamed, I honestly don't care what they think of me. If you don't let yourself care what other people think, you are free and pure. "Life is too big to enclose yourself in the walls of others," he said with a sweet smile on his face. I decided to get up and leave her with her book, but from that day on we chatted occasionally. We were classmates until we graduated from school and I lost track of him. A few years later, his face greeted me smiling in a newspaper photograph. He had just published his second book of stories with very good reviews. It was precisely the life she had imagined since we were in school, and she had achieved it simply by insisting on herself, who she was, and her values.

That is precisely what I would like to invite you to do. Insist on you. On average, human beings live about eighty years. This is a short time in objective terms. Especially since about twenty of those years will be spent in educational institutions and half of all our life time will be spent resting. We have little time to enjoy the miracle of being alive. Do you want to spend it trying to be a person you are not to please others? Remember something simple: if the people around you don't like your essence, it's time to change your environment. I do not want to defend your defects, I only intend to praise your qualities and defend them to the detriment of the criticism they may receive. A few years ago I had an argument with a friend who made fun of me for always being on time for meetings. What's your problem? I told him. Would you like me to be late? Instead of criticizing me for my virtues, you should review your scale of values. Never criticize or make fun of someone for doing things well. Think about this with the eyes of a child: if you make fun of a child for being himself, you are likely to create trauma and make him ashamed of his positive qualities.

RECIPES TO BE YOURSELF

It is somewhat curious to establish a series of recipes and recommendations for a person to preserve their essence. Wouldn't it be enough to simply be? Unfortunately, the current context presents us with a series of absurd social impositions in which we are invited to seek to be different from who we are. The idea has been established that we must be a certain way, betraying our values and principles. This, in the long run, ends badly because only spontaneity has enough strength to transcend. To preserve your essence I will give you some tips.

1.- Acceptance

You are who you are and you must accept yourself. This does not mean that you abandon the obligation to improve every day, but you cannot play a role as if it were a play. If you are an introvert, pretending otherwise will be obvious and will be imposed. Being a fake or projecting discomfort is much more repulsive than the naturalness and calmness of being yourself.

2.- You have not come to please anyone

There are people who live their lives based on the wishes of others. After time, they realize that they have stopped doing what they wanted to do to please others. But time does not recover and the disappointment of having lived the lives of others will accompany them until the end of their days. Pleasing others has a degree of satisfaction as long as you don't abandon your essence and do what you want. You must do what you want with your time, otherwise you will only reach the port of sadness.

3.-Natural

Spontaneity is the basis of being authentic. You must act as your heart tells you, taking care not to impose yourself or disguise rudeness as an absurd form of honesty. Act natural and don't put on costumes or play roles, you are who you are, stay that way.

4.- Don't think about what others think

One of the reasons why some people have trouble being themselves is that they constantly think about "what they will say." Get over this. You cannot live your life conditioned by the vision of others. This will make you a slave. Remember the words of the wise Lao Tzu: "Worry about what other people think, and you will always be their prisoner."

5.- Honesty

Be consistent with your words and actions. If you say something, stick to it, otherwise don't say it. I met a guy who had a penchant for throwing out absolutist phrases and value judgments about everything. I once heard him rant against infidelity - something very questionable, of course -, after a few weeks it was found out that he had been cheating on his wife with a lover for months.

Be honest with words and actions, so you will be sure to always be you.

6.- Get to know yourself

A first step to being yourself is, obviously, knowing who you are. There is a list of values and traits in your personality accumulated since your earliest childhood. It is important that you reflect on them and the values that govern your life today. Are you living what you believe? Are you faithful to your ideals? Or perhaps, to begin you could ask yourself the question: What are my values and ideals?

After identifying these things and being clear about the parameters that govern your life, love them and love yourself. Love yourself because only those who are capable of loving themselves will be able to have the appreciation of others. We are all different, embrace that difference and your particularities, they are precisely the things that make you special. Don't put them aside in pursuit of a feigned personality that, in its attempt to please others, displeases itself.

If you appreciate yourself and your values and qualities, you will have no problems trusting yourself. This is a fundamental step to get closer to the person you are. It is normal to have doubts, in fact, certainties are just disguised signs of weakness. Don't live your life comparing yourself to others. Trust yourself and who you are. If the environment is hostile to you, the problem is not you.

7.- Stay away from pessimism

It is common to find negative thoughts on the path to self-knowledge. People have a tendency to think the worst, this is an evolutionary inheritance, since our brain is designed to protect us in moments of danger. However, the environment has changed a lot and today there are few dangers that nature poses for us. What's the worst that could happen? If you are afraid of being mocked for being yourself, perhaps you should think that it is much sadder to be a slave to fears.

8.- Mistakes are lessons

Making a mistake is an opportunity. There are serious errors, but fortunately they are the minority. Take advantage of them to get something clean. Learn from them and what doesn't quite fit you. Chances are you made a mistake because you followed a path that does not represent you or your values.

9.- Follow your instincts

It's not about becoming a metaphysical being, just trusting the things you feel deeply inside. Your environment may oppose you, but you must follow the voice of your heart. Don't get carried away by the pressure of others. Only you know what will make you happy. Follow that path.

3 QUESTION YOUR BELIEFS

Since we are little, our environment is bombarding us with life beliefs, with ideas of how things should be and how a person should think. If you stop to reflect, both what you think on a political level, as well as the tastes you have in a lot of aspects, such as whether you like a sport or not, almost always comes from your childhood experiences and the tastes of your family. . From birth we are exposed to a series of stimuli that have been filtered by our social environment which, for a long time, is limited to our family. It is a social pact that solidifies over time and is very hard to break, since it implies a break with your inner circle. A traditional example of this is found in the followers of a football team. Almost all the time, a child becomes a fan of a particular team because his father is a fan of the club and has instilled in him a love for the institution. There are very few people who, when they grow up, stop to think and say: "hey, no, in reality Barcelona FC does not represent me and from today I will be a fan of Real Madrid."

This happens with many of the beliefs that we carry within us, their origin is in our family environment and many of them have accompanied us in a thoughtless way. We very rarely question what we believe because we simply consider that all our ideas and beliefs are correct simply because they coincide with those of our family. I know that when reading this some person may think that his political ideas are diametrically opposed to those of his father, however, that person is not taking into account that his political ideology probably corresponds to another family, that of his social environment created from of adolescence. With this I do not mean that whether or not we agree with our family in all aspects makes us different from them or turns us into a carbon copy. What I am trying to propose is that our beliefs are accompanied by a social context from which they arise and at the same time explains them. If a left-wing voter has a right-wing father, it is very likely that his ideology is framed in a group of friends with which he coincides. We relate to the world from a social context that has shaped us and very rarely are we able to distance ourselves from it and reflect on the origin of our beliefs. We go through life as if all our convictions were part of our immovable identity and we often let ourselves be carried away by other people's ideas that we have not worked on intellectually or emotionally. These are often recurring thoughts that do not allow us to fully enjoy our lives.

I invite you to do a little exercise: When was the last time you questioned the origin of the things you think about? Do you think you can review your beliefs? I'm going to tell you a way you can get started.

1. Every time you want someone to react or behave as we consider "appropriate," try to think to whom you are paying tribute. Is what we are asking for really essential for our well-being or does it respond to automatic thoughts? I'm going to give you an example in a simple way: you meet a friend for lunch at a restaurant and during dinner, he puts his elbows on the table. Inside you a voice tells you: "how rude." However, is it really a rude gesture? Does it really bother you or is it your grandmother's voice speaking in your head? Think about it, there are thousands of situations - most of them deeper - in which questioning the origin of your feelings can help you.

2. When you have an argument - whether with your partner or with your friends or family - try to think about whether you are clinging to your position because you believe it is correct or because you do not accept that there are positions different from yours on a certain issue. Accepting the diversity of positions does not necessarily mean incorporating them into your beliefs, it only helps us live freely. After all, you won't be able to do much to change people to your will. On the other hand, the plurality of visions is what gives

life its spice. Think about it: it would be very boring if everyone thought the same.

3. If you are passionately defending a point of view, try to do a splitting exercise and ask yourself for a second whether your interlocutor may feel threatened or attacked by your attitude. If you think this may be the case, your emphasis or irritation when arguing may be related to things outside your point of view. On the other hand, remember that offending will never be an effective way to convince someone.

4. When you are in a group, you may feel uncomfortable because of the apparent homogeneity of thought of the collective. This is because we assume that we must think the same as others to feel comfortable, however it is important to understand that we can share activities without needing to think the same way as others.

5. Thoughts are not a condemnation. What you think today can change tomorrow, you don't need to tie yourself to an idea just because you once believed in it. Part of intellectual evolution involves changing your mind along the way. The same can happen with other people. Talk to others to contrast visions, be open to listening and processing what they tell you.

6. Don't be harsh on yourself. People often judge themselves harshly for thinking a certain way. Do not do it. Be gentle with yourself, the ideas you have may vary or be wrong, there is nothing wrong with that.

7. Don't be afraid of freedom. If you tie yourself to an idea, you become a slave to it. It is true that there are higher ideas, such as respect for freedom or tolerance. But many of the ideas we have can turn us into slaves without it being worth it. Carry your ideas in the pocket of lightness. Be aware that they can change and you will feel freer. Do not lock yourself in the prison of a supposed "consequence" with a thought that you no longer believe in.

LIMITING BELIEFS

Within the universe of things that we believe, there are some perceptions of reality that hold us back in our growth process in various areas of our life, whether spiritual, work, emotional or even as people. I like to see this process as that of a wheat harvester, those enormous machines that go through the fields lifting all the plants, without discrimination. Weeds often sneak in between the beautiful ears of wheat and must be discarded. This is our learning process in the wonderful journey of living. Just as we have heard that we are unstoppable and that we have no limits, we may have heard that we are reluctant when it comes to developing a certain task, without even having dedicated time to practicing it. And so, with that false idea, we convince ourselves that we are not good at something, consolidating a limiting belief that sets a ceiling above us and prevents us from moving forward. Let's not forget that our mind creates realities. That is why if you start thinking about a catastrophic situation that has not happened, your brain will convince itself that it is real and you will feel sad and distressed. Then it is necessary to review and extend, as if they were dirty laundry, our limiting beliefs to analyze whether they are based on facts or are simply the product of a series of fallacies sustained over time.

I would like to use a cliché to continue: belief is power. This phrase encompasses an entire universe of truths, but its frequent use has made it lose its meaning, like when we repeat a word ad nauseam and its mere pronunciation seems strange to us, as if it were melting in our mouth: bread, bread, bread, bread, bread, bread. But believing is power. The first step of any progress is in your mind and in order to take it you must undress yourself from limiting beliefs.

The famous Spanish painter Pablo Picasso once said that if you can dream it, you can create it. There is nothing more certain: triumphs begin with the conviction that they can be achieved. Then we are going to work on everything that limits us.

I invite you to do a practical exercise. Take a notebook or a piece of paper and write on it all the things you think you are not capable of doing. Do not skimp on topics, always taking care of relevance. If you say you're not able to fly, I think you should get yourself checked. If you say that you are not capable of playing soccer at a professional level and you are of a certain age, you may not be understanding the point of the exercise. I am referring to the things that have accompanied you since your early childhood as a conviction: I am not able to dance, I am not able to speak in public, I am not able to ask for a raise in salary, I am not able to use a computer, this of mathematics is not for me.

Next to each of the things you have written, I want you to write a column called: Why? and in it you try to find the basis that explains why you have written that activity there. Next to this, a new column that will be called Did I try it? and answer yes or no, depending on the case.

You will probably realize that many of the things written there have been so foreign to you for so many years that you don't even remember why you think you are not capable of carrying them out successfully. What's more, it is possible that you have never tried to do them, since from a very young age you created a personality that incorporated those limitations as part of its identity. Do you really believe that your personality is something immobile that is not worth revising? Continuing with the practical exercise, I want you to register a new column in which you write: Would I like to try it? and respond accordingly. It is possible that many of the things you think you cannot do are extremely attractive to you but you have not had the courage to go for them because you have believed for many years that they are out of your range. This is a fundamental mistake, since you cannot know if you have the capabilities for something without having tried it. What's more, you cannot evaluate your capabilities for something without having trained in that subject. Do you perhaps believe that great speakers were born with that gift? No, many of them have spent long hours practicing and training the ability to address an audience so they can do it without hesitating or going blank. If this is your case, I recommend that you look for the movie The King's Speech.

WHERE DO THESE LIMITING BELIEFS COME FROM?

It is likely that the practical exercise that I proposed has made you think about the origin of your limiting beliefs, but it is still good that we analyze the origin. Most of these fallacies have been installed in us since our childhood and are due to specific and traumatic situations. Some people believe that they cannot speak in public because when they were children they had a bad time during a school presentation, or they think that they do not have many opportunities with dancing because in their childhood a misplaced relative made fun of their way of moving their body. The words that children hear can be decisive for the rest of their lives and the verbal abuse that an infant receives can be harmful to the development of their personality. This is not to say that all children who hear criticism become troubled beings, but they are much more likely to develop trauma than a person who has grown up in an environment of love, support and encouragement.

It is often said that no one can make you feel inferior without your consent. This is true in most cases, but there are people who are helpless because they grew up in hostile environments, without love or positive reinforcement. It is the duty of parents to encourage their children.

It is important that we know how to differentiate between reality and perception. Reality has a special peculiarity: it has as many versions as there are human beings alive. In this way, people only have our point of view, an approach to reality based on a long list of experiences and learning accumulated over the years. This does not mean that it is right or wrong, simply that it is ours and that we must accept that we do not know how others think and that, at the same time, our thoughts can diverge a little from reality due to the conditioning of information and stimuli. that we have received over the years.

Curiously, our beliefs influence the experiences that have founded our vision of reality and at the same time that vision of reality shapes our beliefs, creating a kind of Moebius ring, an infinite feedback tape into which it is difficult to introduce new information.

It is important to remember that beliefs are nothing more than that: beliefs. They are there because we believe in them, but we can easily stop believing in them and make them disappear. Or we can consolidate them by reinforcing ideas. If I think I can't, I'm lost. If I think I can, well, I will try, I will work, I will train and I will change that belief for a fact: yes I can.

As you will have learned in your experience on earth, people love to be right and we will seek to defend a belief, justifying its bases with facts. If I think I can't write a book, I won't write a book and I'll be right. If you justify your limitations, you will always have some. Don't you think it's time to make mistakes in a good way and break negative beliefs with a dose of effort?

The role of the subconscious in the formation of beliefs is fundamental. If we were children who grew up hearing things like that women should not do certain jobs, it is possible that we are adults with a high degree of machismo that we may find difficult to eradicate, since these thoughts have taken root in our subconscious and are part of our vision of life. reality". But remember: what you consider "reality" is just your interpretation of the world and it may be wrong. Even more so if it involves assigning absurd gender roles.

END LIMITING BELIEFS

Studies have determined that around 60,000 thoughts pass through our minds a day. Most of them are negative in nature. This is not all bad: our brain is designed to protect us from danger, so it imagines negative scenarios, trying to keep us safe from possible threats. However, the world around us has changed faster than the evolution of our brain. Nowadays nature is not a threat to us nor are there large predators lurking to eat us. So it is important that we view those thoughts with distance and analyze their validity. Is it justified to be afraid when the chances of something bad happening are minimal? No, it is not justified or healthy.

Within these catastrophic thoughts, negative beliefs are also installed. Our brain tends to tell us that we shouldn't risk doing something because doing it is more dangerous than not doing it. Doing involves risks that he does not want us to take because he protects us from dangers. But… those dangers no longer exist! What's the worst that can happen if I dare to dance? Make an ass of oneself? Ha! That can even be fun if you know how to take it with humor. Our worst fears are based on crazy situations that have nothing to do with reality. However, we continue to fertilize the field of terror to "keep ourselves safe."

It is important that we define the fields in which limiting beliefs usually occur:

-Lack of faith, when we believe that it is impossible to achieve our goal, we are so sure that it will be impossible that we even doubt trying.

-We are not able. The goal is achievable but not for us, our capabilities are limited and not enough to get there.

-I do not deserve it. Many people give up seeking success because they believe that they do not have the merits for it and they believe that it is reserved for others with more merits.

As you can deduce, these are all mental constructs based on fallacies. However, you will be able to go as far as you think you are capable.

Now that we are aware that these are mental constructions, we must begin the demining process. Limiting beliefs must be constantly challenged, as gradual progress will be the food to continue challenging them until they are eliminated. The evidence of the possible will show you that absurd ideas are worth rooting out.

We can do a new practical exercise similar to the previous one. Now we will take a piece of paper or a notebook and write what facts prove each belief. For example, if we believe that we are not suitable to lead a group, is there something to prove it? Have we tried leading teams in the past? Is there any precedent to prove otherwise? Write it down and your memory will likely show you that you wrongly believe in limiting ideas. On the same sheet I would like you to write a reflection in which you analyze what it is useful for you to have this belief. Is there any value in continuing to believe that? Does it help you to believe that you can't do something? I would like you to also analyze the price you pay for keeping that belief with you. For example, there are people who, at twenty-five years old, believe that they are too old to study a university degree. Years pass and after the blink of an eye they realize that they are thirty years old, they have not studied or done much. They were not old nor are they then, but they have paid a high price for letting time pass without making a decision. Think about the price you pay for your limiting beliefs, there you can find the strength to eradicate them.

In the reflections you are having about limiting beliefs, I would like to invite you to identify the supposed benefits that these ideas give you. They can be in the form of consolation or placebo, since many of the limitations that we believe we have are based on these supposed benefits. Often, the comfort of not taking risks is enough as a "benefit" to continue believing that we cannot carry out a certain task. Think about all the excuses you give yourself to hold on to that idea and try to analyze if they are really as good as you think. Very often we believe that comfort is more pleasant than risk, since it does not imply the possibility of turbulence. But a life lived that way is no longer a life. The monotony of excuses will not help you move anywhere and in the long run, the feeling of frustration will come and you will only be left with the painful question: What if I had tried? I hope you don't get there when it's too late.

My invitation is that you live under a concept: "challenge". Challenge yourself and your limiting beliefs. Every time one of them pokes its nose into your thoughts, look it in the eyes and tell it it's not true. It is not true that you are too old, it is not true that you cannot lead a group, it is not true that you do not deserve success nor is it true that you cannot achieve a goal. It will only be true if you allow it to exist. Think of these beliefs as an evil imaginary friend that will only be there if you let it. Remember how useless it is and that its contribution is only negative: prepare yourself mentally from the beginning of your day with positive ideas that motivate you to achieve everything that your beliefs prevent you from.

I know that this is not achieved overnight, that is why I am talking to you about a daily process, it is a job for which you must be committed and consistent. It is no use believing today to abandon tomorrow. To the extent that you insist on the possibility of changing your beliefs, they will change, but you must be constant and prepare to challenge the identity you created on pillars of sand.

To close this chapter, I would like to leave you with some quotes from famous people in history that can help you find the motivation to challenge your beliefs.

"No one can make you feel inferior without your consent." —Eleanor Roosevelt

"It's not about whether they're going to knock you down, it's about whether you're going to get up when they do." —Vince Lombardi, American football coach

"How wonderful it is that no one has to wait even a second to start improving the world." —Anne Frank

«The pessimist sees difficulties at every opportunity. The optimist sees opportunities in every difficulty." —Winston Churchill

"Don't let your past take up all of your present" —Will Rogers

"What matters is not what happens to you, but how you react to it." —Epictetus

"Sometimes you don't know the value of a moment until it has become a memory" —Dr. Seuss

"Many think about changing the world, but almost no one thinks about changing themselves." —Leo Tolstoy

"It is not death that you should fear, but never begin to live." —Marcus Aurelius

"We may suffer many defeats but we must not be defeated" —Maya Angelou

"The moment you want to quit is just the moment you have to keep moving forward" —Anonymous

"If you're working on something you really care about, no one has to push you: your vision pushes you." —Steve Jobs

"Creativity is intelligence having fun" —Albert Einstein

«You don't have to be big to start. But you have to start to be great." —Zig Ziglar

"Dont wait. "It's never going to be the right time." —Napoleon Hill

"Surround yourself with people who believe in your dreams, encourage your ideas, support your ambitions, and bring out the best in you" —Roy T. Bennet

"No matter what people tell you, words and ideas can change the world" —Robin Williams

"You are never too old to set another goal or have a new dream" —CS Lewis

4 DON'T CREATE PROBLEMS, SOLVE THEM

A few years ago a colleague shared a story with me that stuck in my memory and that I would like to resurface with you today. My friend, a behavioral psychologist with extensive experience in therapy, received a middle-aged man who wanted treatment with him. "Doctor, for some years I feel like I have turned into a crab. I'm only walking backwards and the things that until a while ago were simple for me have become an impossible mountain to climb," said the man who introduced himself as a Harvard engineer with postgraduate studies. Without a doubt, he was a very studied guy with extensive professional and academic preparation. Despite this, the man felt that his life had become an ordeal because as the days went by, making decisions became increasingly complicated. By the time he arrived at my colleague's office, the guy had lost his job and was about to face a divorce, as those around him had lost patience after months of tolerating a lackadaisical attitude towards simple decisions. Still, the poor man found it impossible to get up from his chair and perform. According to my colleague, it was as if from one moment to the next someone had deactivated the hippocampus in his brain, which is essential for decision-making. After talking for a while, they agreed that the man would visit him twice a week and that they would start therapy to treat his illness. However, my colleague wanted to know something before the man left his consultation. "There is something that I do not understand. If you have lost that ability, how come you are here? It takes a lot of willpower to go to the psychologist and you, who tell me that you have lost this ability, appear in my office on your own." The man shrugged his shoulders and replied: "I've hit rock bottom. It was either this or jump out the window."

The poor man suffered from a mental disorder known as aboulomania. This name may not be familiar to you, but it is a more common pathology than some believe. It is basically the inability to make decisions. Sure, many people may consider themselves indecisive or insecure, but this disease takes things into an obsessive field to the point of blocking people, as was the case with my friend's patient.

It is a somewhat extreme pathology, but in practice it helps us address a fundamental issue in people with good mental and emotional health: the ability to solve problems and make practical decisions. There is no doubt that a vitamin person knows very well how to make decisions - they will not always be correct, after all they are a human being - and carry out the actions they must take. So, you're probably wondering: what can we do to be decisive people?

The decisive personality, like many traits in a person's character, can be trained. You just need a strong commitment to your goals and mentality to be able to focus on what is important. We often waste time complaining about our problems instead of solving them. I have news for you that you probably already know but don't want to understand: complaints get you nowhere.

Let's see: complaints are an internal discourse with which we try to alleviate our pain or discomfort with the intention of putting the weight of a failure on another person or condition.

In principle, it is not wrong to complain if there is a justification or the complaint has a functional role, since it can help us receive attention and support, as we can see in the case of babies and their forms of communication before learning to speak our language. language. However, there are also dysfunctional complaints or lead complaints, as I like to call them, because they only sink us into misery, charging us with negative energy without helping us find solutions. They only produce displeasure and stress among those close to us.

So, the first thing you should do when faced with the prospect of complaining is to ask yourself if it is appropriate and if it is of any use.

Complaining to the railway authority because a train did not arrive on time can mean a refund of a ticket, but complaining to your partner because it is raining is so useless that I am not going to detail it.

Why do we complain?

It is a costume
we learned it
Because we are pessimists
It's a topic of conversation
Because we are perfectionists
We are not empathetic
We follow the negativity of others

In short, most of the time we complain pointlessly. Well, does the weather change if I complain? Are my regrets a way of turning back time?

Constant complaining, in addition to not solving the problems that cause it, means entering the hurricane of negativity, clouding our vision of life from a dark and, obviously, negative prism. How heavy! This only creates a bad environment around us, instead of being a vitamin person we become the "polluting" person, who dirtyes everything with his bad face and an attitude that is difficult to bear. Who wants to have someone like that around? Neither you nor anyone, no one. It's logical: would you want to be friends with Luis, the bitter one? I don't believe it. When it comes to choosing who to have coffee with, I'm sure you would prefer Miguel, the cheerful one.

But the biggest problem with living under the auspices of complaints is that we simply do not resolve the situations that generate them. Complaints do not teach us a lesson or invite us to learn new ways to face a conflict; they are like the island of consolation and disappointment. How boring to live like this!

So I invite you to evaluate situations every time the ghost of complaint rears its nose. It's worth it? Change something? Is the momentary relief it gives me enough to live in it? Surely not, so get up and walk, Lazarus. By stopping complaining we will have a better mood and that, if you don't know, I'll tell you, translates into a better state of health. In addition, we will adopt an active attitude to solve day-to-day problems and we will have a much more pleasant reception in our environment. Who doesn't love an optimist? But, above all, stopping complaining means taking responsibility and this is very powerful in building solutions to problems and, ultimately, in modeling a reactive and solid personality.

You must identify your complaints and the reason. Not the reason that generates them but why you complain. Pay attention to the tone in which you speak, if it is angry or sad, it could be that you are complaining. You should also identify the issues you are complaining about, you will probably come to the conclusion that they are usually always the same.

Let's solve problems

Now that we know that complaining is a heavy burden that no one wants to carry, let's act. Generally, complaints arise from day-to-day problems and are a mattress on which to sleep, believing that it is useful for something. But it's not like that and you know it, so let's get to work.

1.- What is the problem?

To learn to be decisive we must learn to recognize problems. You must become an expert in analyzing situations. Because just as it can be a problem not to make a decision, it can also be a problem to make a hasty decision.

2.- What options do you have?

Problems do not have a single correct way to be addressed. Faced with a situation that requires a decision, analyze your options. Take a cold look at the paths you can follow and where each one will take you. Don't spend hours on it, but don't rush it either. Time and practice will give you mastery.

3.-Get informed

To make decisions you must have information. Don't take a path without knowing where it will lead you, try to gather as much information as possible before your verdict.

4.- Are there other paths?

You almost always have other ways to get to a point. Evaluate the relevance of your options. A few years ago I met a woman so methodical that she made comparative tables with her suitors. You don't have to do it, just think about the alternatives.

5.- Do you have the ability to do it?

It is important that you know your capabilities and limitations when making a decision. If you find yourself unemployed and think that an option is to dedicate yourself to professional football, I doubt that it is a good path. The decision you make at all times must be supported by a series of tools that make it possible. Trust in your abilities and lean on them, but don't decide things that are on the sidelines.

6.- Control impulses

Being reactive does not mean that you should act automatically when faced with a stimulus or situation. Many times reactivity is based on the ability to analyze and make a decision. Each situation is different and it is clear that if you have to turn the steering wheel of your car to avoid an accident you have to do it in fractions of a second, but the same does not happen if you have to decide whether it is a good idea to quit your job.

7.- Analyze the risks

The only way to avoid the risks is to hide in a cave and not leave there. Being alive is a risk and making decisions is precisely that, risky. Before making a decision, analyze what can go right and what can go wrong. It is about foreseeing the possible consequences of the decisions we make and making a balance between what you could obtain with that path.

8.- Trust yourself

It is very likely that the decision you have to make is part of a larger general framework that is fairly familiar to you. Trust your experience, remember the moments in the past that have some similarity with the situation you live in today, it is likely that you will find some practical teaching in what happened long ago. If you don't find it, don't stop trusting. Trust is the first step.

9.- Limit the influence of others

It is very good to trust others and consult their opinion if you wish, but what cannot happen is to allow yourself to be bowed down by social pressure. The decisions you make under this influence will not be yours, but you must be the one to assume the consequences.

10.- Act in line with your values

If you want your decisions to leave you happy and in some way feel like they represent you, regardless of whether things go well or badly, it is important that whatever path you choose is in line with your values. Many people believe that the right way to achieve something is to betray their values, this will only ruin their hearts, even if things turn out well. Think, for example, of someone eager to make money who commits a crime. If their values are contrary to this fact, money will not be able to appease the remorse.

Basis of reactivity

Making decisions, doing things, getting going... are issues that require certain personal characteristics that I would like to delve into here with you, after all we are on a journey to get closer to that type of personality.

Creativity:

One of the fundamental characteristics of people with the ability to solve problems is their willingness to invent things every day. If they do not invent something new, they improve what already existed by applying a different vision, after all they are there to solve. In another part of this book I will delve into creativity, but for now I would like to highlight its importance when making decisions.

The optimism

Someone happy is someone ready to act. Optimism is an attitude towards life. If you start the day from a good disposition, it is very likely that you will find a way to solve problems, since attitude can define your direction. An optimist does not give up or get stressed if he faces a problem, it is just another challenge and at the end of the day, these people are collectors of defeated challenges. If things don't go as expected, optimists will see it as a lesson.

They don't give up

A new project or a decision without precedent requires courage. That is why decisive people are usually tenacious. They don't give up and get back up after every setback.

They keep calm

To have a clear mind and be able to make correct decisions, or even just make decisions, it is important to stay calm, even if you find yourself in a moment of great pressure. Whoever loses his cool will be overwhelmed by the situation and will probably get stuck.

Space for criticism

A reactive person is open to constructive criticism, because he knows that this is a way of learning and with the vision of others, added to his own, he can achieve a combination that gives a good result. Without a doubt, the nature of the criticism that a reagent accepts must be relevant. No one can accept criticism that is unjustified or intended to destroy.

fall and get up

It doesn't matter how many stumbles you suffer, the important thing is how many times you are willing to get up. That's what being decisive is all about, having the ability to try again and again.

They take the initiative

Decisive people were not born to become a chorus of voyeurs who support a leader's decisions. These are precisely people with initiative, especially in difficult times. This is why, beyond solving problems, they become leaders of their social groups, because they do not wait for anyone to tell them things, they act on their own.

5 Forgiveness and forgetting

After the fall of the Latin American dictatorships, many victim groups coined the slogan "Neither forgiveness nor forgetfulness." The phrase made a lot of sense for all those who considered the idea of a clean slate impossible with those who until recently applied the bloodiest torture to their relatives for having different political views. After the arrival of democracy in Chile, President Patricio Aylwin of the Christian Democracy party, opened a controversy by saying in his inaugural speech that Chilean society should begin a process of unity between civilians and the military, since they were all part of a national unity. . In the midst of a boo when naming the military, Aylwin insisted: "yes, compatriots, Chile is one," turning the shouts into applause. His presidency went down in history as the beginning of a complex process of reconciliation despite the voices that insisted that it should not be forgiven or forgotten.

There is no doubt that forgiving is not easy. A voice resonates within us that tells us that it is impossible to let go of the damage we have suffered. The feeling of injustice drives us to maintain the idea that forgiveness is not possible without fair reparation. This is not entirely correct, much less good for our spirit. Or soul. Or conscience. An ancient Greek phrase defines resentment very precisely: "Hate is like drinking a glass of poison hoping that the other person will die." If you think that by holding that resentment against a person you can change things, you are very wrong. The only one who will suffer is you and that broth of hatred will cook you on many levels, affecting your life in many ways, including your health. Recent studies have shown that hate generates a state of excitement that can produce muscle tension, gastrointestinal discomfort, hypertension and feelings of overload that will affect your body.

We cannot forget that emotions are connected to our body. When we feel anger, we release hormones and substances such as adrenaline, cortisol or prolactin; The longer they are secreted in the body, the more damage the immune system suffers and the body is more susceptible, as Robert Ader, a researcher at the Rochester School of Medicine and Dentistry, explained in a popular science article.

But the thing do not ends there. Research from the Neurobiology Laboratory at University College London revealed that when hate is felt, the central area of the brain, known as the putamen, and the insula, located on the lateral surface, are activated. Interestingly, these are the same areas that are activated when you feel romantic love. It is logical that these parts are stimulated because they are passions that can lead to committing irrational and aggressive acts. This explains why the feeling of hate raises your blood pressure and accelerates your heart rate, making you susceptible to heart disease. Dr. Irina Matveikova, a specialist in endocrinology and clinical nutrition, assures that emotions end up having an effect on the stomach. Tension causes a knot or emptiness in the face of frustration that is somatized or reflected in an illness, to the point of developing a stomach ulcer.

Martin Luther King, the leader of the African American civil rights movement in the United States, once said that "he who is incapable of forgiveness is incapable of love." He, who had suffered firsthand the injustices of a system of racial segregation, invited his community to practice forgiveness as a form of personal growth. Because forgiveness is a form of freedom. Just like love, hate can bind us to a person, but it will do so for dark and negative reasons and we can never be whole if we accumulate hate inside us. Forgiveness involves looking to the future, leaving the past behind because, without a doubt, it is something we cannot change.

Many people mistakenly believe that the act of forgiveness is an act of kindness toward a person who did not act right toward us. This is not entirely true: yes, it is an act of kindness, but towards ourselves. Forgiveness allows us to move forward and be better people to the extent that it frees us from hatred and resentment. But like all the things that build us, it involves effort and dedication.

There are people who oppose forgiveness because they believe that forgiving can expose them to being victims of the same offenses they forgave, or because they believe that compassion and forgiveness can strengthen the aggressor, encouraging him to repeat his bad behavior to get away with it. However, forgiving is an act of self-care, it is a gift that each of us should give ourselves because it will help us become better people and, ultimately, happy.

Of course, forgiveness does not mean that we are masochists and that we accept the evil of others against us with a divine design. Nor is it a synonym for impunity regarding the consequences of bad acts; if a person acts unfairly, they must assume the consequences. Forgiveness means freeing ourselves from the heavy burden of hate and moving forward through life open to new experiences without the fear of being victims. One of the teachers of forgiveness was Nobel Peace Prize winner Nelson Mandela. In an interview, someone asked him how he had managed to forgive the injustice he suffered through his imprisonment and he said: "When I walked through the door I realized that if I continued to hate I would still be in prison."

Can you learn to forgive?

Many people will wonder if we can learn to forgive or if the way we handle our emotions is something that is pre-established in our subconscious as an indelible mark of our personality. The first thing we must know is that we are social beings in constant construction and that one of the things that most societies inherited from the Western tradition teach us is that forgiveness is a divine attribute, worthy of our gods. Within the Catholic structure, it is the priest who delivers forgiveness, as God's intermediary on earth, since ultimately it is God who must forgive our sins. Regardless of one's religious belief, allow me to question this idea from constructive criticism: if God created man in his image and likeness, then that divine forgiveness is also within us. If you are a person who does not adhere to the Catholic religion, this also applies to you: the ability to forgive is also one of our highest samples of rationality, since you will agree with me that it is useless to carry a burden on past situations. that you cannot modify. To the metaphor of poison that I mentioned before, I would like to add one that is attributed to Siddhattha

Gautama, the Buddha, and that defines resentment as an ember that you hold in your hand to throw at another, while you are the one that burns.

To begin the complex process of learning to forgive, I would like to recommend some steps:

Understand the damage that resentment does to us

Once we are victims of an injustice or affront, we think about the damage that another person or a certain circumstance has caused us that is completely out of our control. It is a logical step in the rationalization that our brain makes to try to learn from the situation and draw lessons that, as far as possible, help it avoid putting ourselves in similar situations. Everything good until then. The damage came from outside and it is normal to have reflections about this. However, I would like to invite you to reflect on the damage you cause to yourself when you are not able to forgive and overcome an offense. If we let resentment and anger take over our feelings, they will only grow uncontrollably and severely harm our social relationships. A simple question could help you put things in perspective. Do you know anyone who you can define as bitter? If you answer yes, you will be thinking about what you think of that person and whether you can feel comfortable around them. I'm sure you think that beyond the deep affection you may have for him, his company is not pleasant and from a distance he seems like a person who suffers and whose life is not happy. Precisely in this concept lies the reflection that I want to invite you to have regarding your hatred and resentments: they are a plot against happiness. Often, we tend to believe that happiness is a goal that we must achieve and that it is blocked by a series of factors external to us. This is not the case, but we will delve into that later.

It is important that we always keep in mind that all people have suffered emotional blows and that it is almost impossible not to suffer them, we are alive. But if we allow ourselves to sink into the pit of misery and become slaves to those negative feelings, we will only cause more harm to ourselves. Our brain does not recognize the difference between real sensations and imaginary ones. Let's see, it's a little more complex than this, but you will have already noticed that if you start thinking about the possibility of being mugged, you will suffer from real fear. And that fear makes your body tense and suffer in the same way you would if you were really assaulted. The same thing happens with hate and resentment: feelings from the past sneak into our body to cause physical ailments.

Only you are the owner of your feelings

It is possible that we are not responsible for a negative situation that we have had to experience. We cannot control everything and the mere act of trying to control even part of it is absurd. Since we don't own the situation, let's take charge of how we feel about it. Initially, hate acts as a defense mechanism. Our brain believes that if we generate hatred for a person, it is impossible for them to harm us again in the way they did. That is not entirely true and that hatred will not prevent another different person from harming us in the same way, so it is not effective in its purposes. If we are aware that we have the power to modify these feelings, we can use them so that a negative experience becomes learning and, in the long run, controlling them will help us become the famous vitamin person in our environment.

I propose a simple exercise. The next time you feel offended by a situation. Try not to react too hot. Analyze your feelings, watch them pass before your eyes as if they were a flock of migratory birds. Think about whether the situation warrants all those birds flying in front of you. You may realize that it's not worth feeling things as big as hate for a situation like this. You can also think about it with a situation from the past that you still think about. To illustrate, I will tell you a brief episode I had with a boss at the beginning of my working life. The guy was a dictatorial boss in all his forms and tried to control who was part of his team even outside of work. I showed my opposition to his questions and outbursts and he decided to shout my farewell in front of all my colleagues. I felt humiliated and a victim of a terrible injustice. The situation tormented me for months: I thought about the episode with resentment and anger, reliving his words and gestures, in short, every day I relived what happened until one afternoon I felt a strange abdominal pain that took me straight to the hospital. After a thorough examination, the doctor asked me why I had the pain. I did not understand his question and he told me: "Yes, you have caused an ulcer in your stomach, there is something in your life that torments you and you live bitterly, which has caused a laceration in the walls of your stomach." I knew that it was about my dismissal, in those days everything was about my dismissal and that medical visit was the warning bell that made me see things clearly: if I did not control my thoughts and my feelings, they would take me down a rabbit hole. path of bitterness and pain. I discussed the matter with a colleague from the psychology department who had been my therapist during some university exercises. His words helped me reflect on the unknown power of all humans to control their feelings and focus their lives.

Am I really willing to forgive?

A fundamental step in the process of forgiving is being willing to do so. By now, you know very well that if you are not willing to do a thing, you cannot force yourself to do it. In behavioral psychology we have analyzed this phenomenon and it is usually one of the first things said to an alcohol addict. If you are not willing to let it go, no one can force you. You are the owner of your behaviors and feelings, if you do not control them or take them where you think they should go, they will dominate you in a self-destructive way. Forgiveness is a process that comes from what metaphysics usually calls "the heart." Words can make us believe we are doing something just by naming it. They can be a good first step, but true forgiveness implies a vocation for peace and liberation from those feelings.

A few years ago a man came to my office with serious motivation problems to live his life. He was stuck in a mediocre job and most aspects of his life were not what he said he wanted. As we talked, several of his frustrations came to the surface: he had a boss who did not value his work and his wife had abandoned him, leaving him to care for a teenage son with school problems. In his words it was clear that he believed he was a victim: of his boss, of his wife and of society. As our therapy progressed, I realized that the man had adopted that victim role as a justification for his failures. Since the world had been evil, he had the "right" to fail without being called out for his negligence towards himself. Hatred of those who had offended him was the perfect excuse for not taking charge of his life. After a few sessions he told me that he did not plan to continue with the therapy: "I am not willing to forgive anyone for what they have done to me, you believe that I am to blame for my misfortunes, without taking into account that I am a victim of circumstances," he told me. "I think you own your circumstances and feel comfortable in the role of victim. After all, it is quite easy to stay down and blame others," I replied. He looked at me with surprise and contempt. I had hit the mark and he knew it, but he was not willing to take the first step to take control of his life, so he got up and left my office upset. I am probably now part of the long list of people who have made him a "victim."

Express yourself

Forgiveness doesn't mean that your feelings are swept under the rug. On the contrary, the process towards forgiveness and forgetting offenses should be the opposite: it is a path in which you must express your feelings and not hide them, only then can you feel that what happened made you reflect and grow as a person. . You need to clarify your ideas, write them down or talk about them with someone in your circle of trust. Expelling everything we feel will make us feel lighter and help us release the burden of hate. Given this recommendation, a dilemma arises: should I express myself to the person who hurt me? Not necessarily. First you must express yourself to yourself to know your feelings and then you can decide whether or not it is worth confronting your aggressor. Many times you will see that it is not necessary and that once you have clarified your ideas and discussed them with a loved one, confronting the person is not necessary. However, sometimes it will be therapeutic to be able to communicate to a person the harm they did to us and how they made us feel. The danger of this is falling into a spiral of conflict or finding ourselves with answers that only increase the pain. Remember that the process of forgiveness is mainly an act of love towards you, a gesture of liberation that will make you a better person.

An exercise that we usually propose in our therapies has been used by humanity for millennia: write a letter to the person who has offended you. Try to be as honest as possible, don't hold anything back, be clear and open, explain how you feel and why you feel that way. Don't be afraid to be impulsive or overdo it as long as you can express in detail how you feel. It is not necessary for you to send the letter, I assure you that the writing process will have been so rewarding and liberating that it will not be necessary to confront your attacker. Remember that resentment and hatred create a personal bond. Paradoxically, when a person hates another, they think much more about them than if they were indifferent, creating that toxic bond.

Mirror

Learning to forgive can be a little easier if we learn to know ourselves, if we accept who we are and how we are. Although no human being is the same as another, we belong to the same species and have the same hereditary genetic traits, so our behaviors can be repeated. This is what social sciences are based on: the patterns and repetitions in our behavior as a sign that we come from a common origin that over hundreds of thousands of years of evolution forged a character.

This is why the mirror is an important tool when learning to forgive. A little empathy can help you understand a person's reasons for acting in a certain way and thus realize that we probably could have acted the same way if we were in their place.

Resentment and suffering often conspire against our ability to see things clearly. They are poisonous feelings that cloud our reason. Fueled by sadness, rejection, humiliation and disappointment, resentment and suffering make us forget that, like the person who hurt us, we are also human beings with the capacity to generate that same pain in others. Accepting our potential evil is an act of justice that makes us better people. No one is exempt from sin and accepting it humanizes us.

Putting yourself in the place of the person who hurt you will help you change your perspective on the event. Not only because you will see their reasons, but because you will realize that you could have done the same. We are used to judging and we miss the context, seeing that we can also have negative behaviors in a given situation will help us take the weight off our resentment.

It's not about justifying your attacker. There are behaviors that could never be validated regardless of the context, it is about understanding that our actions are only a part of us and unfortunately you had to encounter a negative action from a person. Nothing else.

Loose

Let's go back to the Buddha's idea: hate is a burning ember that you hold in your hand to throw at someone. Meanwhile it burns you. Hate only hurts those who feel it. Many times the object of that contempt is unaware of him and lives his life quietly because, after all, he has forgotten his offense. Letting go is a fundamental step in forgiveness. Does it help to remember every day that ten years ago you were fired from your job? No, unless you want to make an old joke that says: "thirteen years and two months ago they called me spiteful." Okay, it's not very funny and it's even less funny when you realize that wear and tear is on your side. To the sadness of many people, the past does not exist. It is a time that we cannot transform and that if we insist on stagnating in it, it will transform us, closing the doors of the future.

How to learn to let go? It is important to play and look at life from outside of ourselves. Every time a spiteful thought enters your head, try to identify why it got there and if it helps if you are sorry. As time goes by, you will have better control over your ideas and feelings and you will be able to prevent negative fantasies - those in which you relive an argument or create a series of imaginary responses to a past conflict - from taking up valuable time in your life.

Generosity and humility

Learning to forgive requires work that will make you great in other areas of your life. It's about generosity. Don't expect forgiveness to offer you things in return beyond that personal growth. This is already a big profit. Generosity will turn you into a vitamin person who will have a series of emotional rewards that nothing can buy. But do it without expecting the person you forgave to reward you in some way. Because forgiving also requires using humility. Forgiving does not give you moral superiority over the person who hurt you. What's more, if what you are looking for is to show your attacker that you are better than him, you are taking the wrong path. If you forgave it is because you consider that it is not worth staying with that mistake, it is because you believe that you can move on and what you learned from the experience will make you grow.

Damage control

Within large organizations, when a problem occurs, a series of protocols are established to identify its cause and resolve its consequences; this process is usually called damage control. It is about identifying exactly what happened, why it happened and what consequences it will have. It seems to me that human beings should practice this process to the point of incorporating it into our lives.

Since all of this is better understood without abstractions, I am going to give an example to help me explain it. If we take the case of a person who suffers from his partner's infidelity, the situation may put him under extreme pressure. Feelings of disappointment, humiliation, deception, and contempt could take over him or her, bringing his or her self-esteem to the ground suddenly. The situation is serious, we can't deny it, but if we do some damage control, we can look at things a little more coldly: the person you had been dating for six months has noticed someone else. This can happen to anyone and the deception did not result from a plot to make him suffer, but as part of the selfish and hedonistic behavior of the person who until then was his partner. If we go deeper, this damage control could make us see that what has happened also serves as an opportunity to end a relationship with a person who, given the facts, did not fully appreciate him and despite all the negative feelings, Nothing that made him desirable is gone. Therefore, resentment towards that unfaithful person could only be a waste of time. The damage it has caused is strong but may be brief. So, looking at it from a new distance, the deceived person sees that the damage has been limited and chooses forgiveness as a healthy way to move forward.

You may be wondering how to forgive a betrayal or how to forgive an infidelity. We have seen that there are attitudes that can bring us closer to forgiving from the heart and now we would like to provide a set of advice on how to forgive a specific person, for example, how to learn to forgive your partner, how to forgive a friend, how to forgive someone. a mother or how to forgive someone who has hurt you.

Memento Mori

Memento mori, translated into Spanish as "Remember that you will die", is a mythical Latin phrase that was used to remember our condition as mortals and the transience of life. According to some historians, the phrase originated in Ancient Rome. It is said that when a general paraded victoriously through the streets of Rome, behind him a servant was responsible for reminding him of the limitations of human nature, to prevent him from becoming arrogant and believing himself omnipotent. According to Tertulano's texts, the phrase that was shouted was: "Respice post te! Hominem te esse memento!" which in Spanish says "Look behind you! Remember that you are a man!"

We often forget our condition as mortals and waste time on absurd speculations, on old hatreds, on nonsense from the past that we cannot change. Remember that you belong to the human species, which thanks to the developments of modern medicine lives an average of 80 years and that is very little time to carry hatred in your heart. If you incorporate the transience of life into your thoughts, you will learn not only to forgive but also to take advantage of every moment because in cosmic terms, you no longer exist and being alive is the product of billions of coincidences that some call a miracle. Enjoy it without hate.

Forgive yourself too

When I went to psychology school, everything about self-forgiveness and healing seemed like an absurd story typical of environments that smell of incense. If this is your case, let me tell you a little more. During a conversation with one of my colleagues who works in the behavioral field, I complained about my difficulties socializing with strangers. I felt that breaking the ice with someone to whom I had not been formally introduced was a huge drain on me in many areas and the few times I tried it turned out to be disastrous. The matter was beginning to scare me because I was around thirty years old and I had not managed to establish a serious romantic relationship with people who seemed to be to my liking but who at the same time were unattainable to me because they were strangers, even if we were at the same party.

My colleague looked at me carefully and said:

—Well Bill, I want to ask you a question. What has happened in your life recently that you come to seek help for this today and not before?

His question left me speechless. The guy was right. Why had he waited so many years to seek help? Had my problem gotten worse enough to become urgent? I wouldn't know for sure what led me to ask him about the matter, but in our conversation I said some things that for him were a clear sign of what was happening.

Told me:

—Bill, don't take this the wrong way, but the way you talk about yourself makes it sound like you have a problem with yourself. I think you should explore forgiveness towards yourself. Forgive yourself your mistakes and defects, learn to love yourself in a pure way.

We decided that I would visit him once a week and discuss the matter. Furthermore, he invited me to explore as many aspects of self-forgiveness as I could. Literature on this topic abounds, but I wanted to look for a source that was a little more scientific than the majority of new age pamphlets that were on the market.

I came across an interesting work by Frank D. Fincham and Julie Hall called "Self-Forgiveness: the Stepchild of Forgiveness Research." Something like "Self-forgiveness, the first step in research on forgiveness." The work addresses some topics that I have delved into throughout my life and that I would like to share today.

The ability to forgive oneself is the basis of emotional stability and the key to inner peace. After all, you will have to spend your entire life with yourself, stop feeling guilty for past mistakes and give yourself a hug of reconciliation. It is not easy, but there are some tricks that will help us advance along this path. Before leaving I must say that to travel it requires training in human aspects such as humility, patience, self-esteem and kindness.

I have often heard the logical question on this matter: why should we forgive ourselves? Many people believe that they have no need to carry out a process of self-forgiveness and reunion with themselves, but they spend their lives reproaching themselves for past mistakes without understanding that this is precisely what self-forgiveness consists of: it is about getting rid of a great weight because we are old. mistakes, for behaviors that we do not approve today or for negative feelings that only drag us towards emotional instability. It is normal for us to feel bad for having hurt someone. Otherwise we would have psychopathic traits. The problem is that many times we get stuck in that feeling of guilt without being able to move forward. Guilt works as a learning tool that teaches us every time we do something wrong. If we exceed a behavioral line, it may be that at the moment we fall prey to the impulse and emotion, the euphoria of acting outside the norm, however, soon guilt will tell us that we should not have done that and it will shape our behavior. The problem arises when the doses of guilt are outside the normal range. As I already said, the absence of guilt is a psychopathic trait, but excess guilt can also be very conflictive, especially in relation to our self-esteem. If we feel guilty for all the mistakes of the past, we carry a heavy burden that does not allow us to move forward, as if a huge whirlpool was swallowing our mental stability. If I am guilty of so much, life becomes difficult for me and the past becomes present to us again and again.

What does it mean to forgive yourself?

In the first therapy session, my colleague told me, "Look, I want you to know from the beginning that forgiving yourself doesn't mean you have to justify all your wrong behaviors. Self-forgiveness is not a license to be a bad person without a guilty conscience. Forgiving yourself means that you assume the guilt of the past and can contemplate the feelings they produced in you without letting them live in you every day." I found his words so beautiful that I wrote them in my notebook and they were an invitation to investigate the entire process in more depth.

The first thing I discovered was that forgiveness, both for oneself and for others, is not simple or sudden. To begin the process we must change the perspective we have of the fact that we cannot overcome. It is important to put the situations in context and accept that we cannot modify the past and that we are no longer the same people who made a mistake years ago. In fact, that mistake has probably allowed us to grow as people and we should be grateful for the learning we have learned from it. we take out It's not about making mistakes every day, it's about learning from the ones we will inevitably make throughout our lives.

Process phases:

1. Analyze the source of blame
We have to know the origin of our feelings. If we have lost a partner because we made a mistake, it is essential that we analyze the causes of that mistake. Maybe we were not completely comfortable with our partner, maybe we entered into a toxic relationship where there was room for revenge... there are many factors. The important thing is to be honest with ourselves when identifying the facts that make us feel guilty.

2. Assume the facts
We all know that impunity is an illusion in emotional matters. Actions have a consequence and that is where the problem of guilt often lies. We want pleasure without taking responsibility for the consequences. And on many occasions the consequences are the burden on our conscience that this discomfort generates. You have to take responsibility and face the consequences, it may be hard, but it will alleviate any guilt.

3. Accept emotions

A fundamental step in self-forgiveness is to understand how we felt when we made a mistake. Feelings and emotions are a part of our being that operates irrationally and can give us clues about who we are deep down. Sometimes, guilt is given by what we are supposed to feel and not by what we really feel, the social mold drives us to believe that we should feel something that does not appear anywhere inside us.

4. The time to take responsibility

If you did something you shouldn't have, don't make excuses or hide. Take responsibility for your actions, this will make you brave and allow you to enter the field of self-forgiveness with the banner of dignity.

5. Now, the consequences

If I am responsible for a mistake, the consequences also belong to me. If I committed infidelity, I must accept that this implies the possibility of ending a relationship even if I don't want to. Part of the consequences of many mistakes is knowing that we are responsible for causing pain to loved ones. It's sad, face it, but don't stay there.

6. Why can't I forgive myself?

Try to think about all the things that prevent you from moving forward in life without the burden of having made a mistake. Also think about all the things you can do to let go and forgive yourself. Many times the confession or reparation of the damage is the beginning of the solution.

7. Ask for forgiveness

It doesn't matter if you offended someone else or you offended yourself: ask for forgiveness, even if it's from yourself. You cannot accept a mistake without the intention of repairing it and a fundamental part of repair is asking for forgiveness. Apologize for the abandonment in which you have been or for the absurd hedonism to which you have dedicated your life. Talk to you, listen to yourself.

8. Repair

Whatever you have done wrong, direct your actions to repair the damage caused. I'll give you a close example: one of my great childhood friends gave himself up to drinking and drugs since he was a teenager. He lived by the absurd motto of die young, leave a beautiful corpse. Although to tell the truth, his would be less and less beautiful. Partying and toxins damage the skin and cause premature aging. The truth is that when he turned 38, the man entered a deep depression and sought help. It was clear that his life was torturing him and everything that seemed like a party was actually a prison from which he could not escape. Months of therapy and detox helped him get out of the hole and a couple of years later he was confronted with an obese, emaciated figure in front of the mirror. What did? Well, what he should have done a long time ago, to repair the mistake made with his life and the abuse of his body, he joined a gym and began visiting it daily. After a few months his appearance was impressive. The ways to repair a mistake, with yourself or with others, can be diverse. Explore.

9. Meditate

Meditation has profound benefits on mental health and can be a tool that helps in the process of self-forgiveness. I don't know if you already practice it, but if not, I recommend doing a little research on which technique is best for you. In any case, a good start can be to simply close your eyes, take a deep breath and think about a specific situation that you want to leave behind. Your thoughts will fly and you will be able to have a new perspective.

I will not be a prophet when I say that the path of forgiveness is complex and requires effort. But is there anything in life that doesn't require it? That effort will undoubtedly have a great reward: letting go of the pain and living a life without burdens from the past that oppress us. If we manage to move forward without these moorings, we will be able to decide about our future. Accepting that we were wrong and made a mistake, even if it was unconscious, is taking the reins of our life in a healthy and responsible way. If we let pain decide our course, we are not only being negligent of ourselves, but we will live a life of bitterness. And believe me, that life also leads to loneliness and rejection, fueling a vicious cycle in which no one wants to live.

6 Early listener

I'm going to give you one of my recipes from the first therapy session I do with my patients. You have come here because you are intelligent and you are willing to improve in all aspects of your life that you can and I deduce that you are one of those who use - even without knowing it - that Japanese philosophy that says: Today better than yesterday, tomorrow better than today. It is about Kaizen or change for the better. If you want, we can use one of its most common translations that talks about continuous improvement. We talk about following the flow of life at all its levels from learning and growing every day.

Since you are on this path, I must tell you that learning to listen will help you understand everything. In times where the speed of information ruffles our feathers daily with new things, thousands of banalities and a bombardment of worthless content, learning to listen is a skill that can help us differentiate fine salt from coarse salt and that, In addition, it will make us great people because even though it seems that we are living in the moment of greatest connection and socialization in the history of humanity, the reality is that human beings are increasingly alone behind digital social networks that distance us. of the true social networks, those of our family, our neighborhood, our friends and neighbors.

Listening to others is the key to empathy and, at the same time, it helps us decipher people's contexts, their motivations and feelings, their desires, desires and frustrations. We often tend to judge behaviors and events. The popular saying already says it, actions and not words. However, the words of the other give us a context of that fact that we judge. By listening we can understand the positions of others and their intimate conditions, while it can open our eyes to that open secret: you are not alone in the world and each of the almost eight billion human beings is a universe. per se.

Learning to listen is a fundamental basis for creating bonds. It is, once again, about applying the elementary principle of all human relationships: treating people as you would like to be treated. If you develop the ability to listen openly and without prejudice, you will become a vitamin person that everyone will want to have around and this will work naturally because feeling heard implies feeling validated as a person and recognized as an interlocutor. I'm sure you're thinking about the times you've been in both situations: the automatic affection for the people who listened to you and the feeling of unease for feeling that the people with whom you share your concerns and feelings heard you without listening.

It is likely that you too have received the school lesson to differentiate listening from hearing, but it is also likely that your teachers have forgotten the fundamental difference between the two concepts. It's not just about paying attention, it's about doing it from empathy and free of prejudice because every time we apply a prior judgment, we are not living a person's present. I'm going to give an example: a while ago I met a woman with whom I became close friends. We used to go for walks in the woods and tell each other about our lives. At that time she was embarked on a relationship without destiny and over time, our conversations became a kind of therapy in which she told me how miserable her life was because the man she had married stopped paying her attention. attention. After a while they decided to separate and our conversations became even more filled with their misery and sadness. She complained because nothing in her life was going well and the new men she met seemed to be interested only in sex and not her feelings. After a year of their breakup, I started to distance myself from this woman. I had a sincere appreciation for her, but I felt that our relationship was not balanced, since it only came in one direction: she expressed all her feelings, generally negative, I listened to her and that was the end of the matter. After several years of estrangement, I received an email from him telling me that he had returned to the city and wanted to see me. Initially I had certain doubts. I relived those one-sided conversations full of drama and tragedy in which she seemed to bathe in her own pain. After thinking about it, I decided to accept his proposal and we met in a cafe. On the way to our date, I mentally reviewed what our history had been and my predisposition to our meeting was tangible. Upon arriving at the cafe, I met a radiant woman with a beautiful smile on her face. She greeted me very warmly and in our conversation I met a person completely different from the one I remember of her. She spoke with enthusiasm about life and her professional projects, she had found love with whom he seemed like a wonderful man according to her words and while we talked I thought about the serious mistake I had made by thinking of her as the woman of the past, canceling her ability to improve as a person. This taught me to leave prejudices on the shelf and listen to each person as if it were the first time we spoke, because the present tense is the only one that exists and we all have the right to change.

The logical question you should be asking yourself is: how do I learn to listen? And you are right, we have come to learn. This is a process that could be simple if we apply empathy, as I mentioned a little above. Within the teachings of Gautama Buddha and his followers in the field of what we know today as Buddhism, I would like to rescue the one that tells us about that great internal enemy that is our ego. If you think about your social interactions, often that ego is waiting for the opportunity to make a show and in conversations it appears when instead of listening you are waiting for your interlocutor to pause so you can speak and say something that can lead the conversation. talk towards a terrain where your ego can camp at ease.

I'm going to give you some practical tips to reverse this situation:

Focus on listening without judgment

The first step to learning to listen is not to judge. Put aside your judgments and prejudices and try to pay attention to what the other person says. This doesn't mean you have to agree with what they tell you, but at least let them finish! We often suspect which way the water will go to the mill and try to cut off the speech because we disagree, without allowing the other person to fully state their points of view, and we disrespect them without letting them finish. Likewise, our judgments or prejudices usually impose a great filter that prevents us from opening up to listen fully and causes us to belittle the words of our interlocutor. A classic example of this occurs when a person who fervently believes in a religion and a person who does not profess any creed meet. The prejudices that both parties have cause the other's words to be devalued and the listening process is completely broken. I would like to recommend a book in which this encounter produces quite the opposite, it is The Monk and the Philosopher, where Jean-François Revel and Matthieu Ricard, father and son, one an agnostic philosopher and the other a Buddhist monk, establish an interesting dialogue. about Buddhism that also serves as a great example of listening.

I would like to take advantage of this subtitle to talk about the importance of not insulting your interlocutor. This seems obvious, but in practice it is not, as it happens so frequently that it makes me think otherwise. When you insult a person, their brain develops a self-defense mechanism through which its ability to empathize with you or listen to you is blocked, because it will think that after you have crossed the barrier of respect nothing good can appear there. Curiously, people who want to convince others of a certain idea, let's say for example that their political current is better, start from the insult, nullifying any possibility of "conversion."

Tolerance, patience and flexibility are fundamental pillars for learning to listen, because even if we do not agree with what we hear, the ability to internalize those words and transmit that openness to our interlocutor will create an important bond.

active listening

For me and many of my fellow psychologists, this tool is the foundation for learning to listen. As I explain what it is, you may think that some of these things you already knew or have even tried to apply them in the past. You're right. Paradoxically, in the complex path to becoming a better person, many of the tools are part of common sense. And if it is so common, why is it not exercised?

Personally, I like to define active listening as "being present." Many times we find ourselves in a conversation and our brain is wandering about other matters, perhaps thinking about the things we have to do when we get home or early tomorrow when we return to work. That is certainly not listening. But it is not being present either. To actively listen to an interlocutor we have to use our full awareness and use tools such as our own body. This is very simple: active listening helps us establish a bridge of intimacy with other people that is only possible if they recognize our complete attention in their words. To do this we have our body attitude and our gestures. Think, for example, about how you feel every time you speak to a person and they do not establish eye contact with you. Well, you're not the only one.

But before making this type of connection, I would like to recommend something that is often left out of texts about the importance of listening. The first step to being a fair and empathetic interlocutor comes long before entering into a conversation with another person. It's about learning to listen to yourself. If you don't know how to listen to yourself, it is very difficult for you to learn to listen to others. Remember that you are the person with whom you will spend your entire life and paying attention to yourself is essential for this and many other things. I would like to recommend that you flirt with what today they usually call "mindfulness" and that I like to maintain in Spanish under the concept of full attention. Try to look at your thoughts as if they were birds crossing the sky, so you can see them from a certain distance, without judgments or evaluations. Avoid external noises that we often use to silence our thoughts. Yes, I mean turning on the TV or radio or even going on social media. They are noises that take you away from yourself. Sport is another very powerful tool to be in touch with yourself, as it disconnects you from everything external.

If you think that you have overcome this phase and throughout your life you have been in contact with your inner voice or are working on it, we can move on to talk about active listening itself. Many people think that this is an empty concept that is based simply on actively paying attention. However, it is something a little more complex that requires a significant cognitive effort, because as you may have heard, attention is a limited resource and people tend to have what some educators call "the attention curve," which involves a period of greater ability to understand what we hear until our brain gets tired and asks for a break. This is likely to transport you back to your time as a student, where after a certain time classes seemed eternal, according to a study by the University of California, the time that can be dedicated to direct instruction for students varies between 5 to 8 minutes for first and second graders and amounts to between 12 and 15 minutes for seniors. But there is hope: attention can be trained with these basic tips:

To meditate
Do exercise

Take notes by hand
Stay hydrated
Ask questions
Listen to music
Drink tea

This not only applies to active listening, but it can certainly strengthen your skills in this field.

A fundamental idea in active listening is to understand that all human beings are a mystery. If we manage to internalize this idea we will be awakening to the virus of curiosity, an important part of attention. If we understand that we all have something interesting to say, it is likely that our interest in their words will grow, enhancing our capacity as listening beings.

I started this chapter with a logical deduction regarding your interest in learning and following that path I must assume that you are one of the people who likes to discover the mystery that others suppose. Remember that the only people who learn nothing are those who believe they know everything and who demonstrate their ignorance through the arrogance that this entails. A phrase frequently attributed to Albert Einstein states that "the ignorant criticize because they believe they know everything, the wise respect because they recognize that they can learn something new."

Active listening also has a non-verbal dimension that I find extremely interesting. It's about being so present that you try to hear what the person is trying to express without speaking. Your feelings, ideas and thoughts implicit in your words. Many times we want to say more than what we express with our voice and the key to understanding this underlying message is empathy and reading gestures.

In practical terms, active listening is accompanied by signals that keep the link active, such as verbal communication, which is known as the phatic function of language and is composed of constant feedback on attention. That is, interjections like "I see, I understand, umm, aha." Non-verbal language is also present, such as eye contact, gestures that react to the other's words or the disposition of the body.

In addition to gestures such as nodding your head, a good idea is to briefly repeat, and from time to time, what your interlocutor is saying. This will help you follow the thread of the conversation without getting distracted, and will increase the other person's confidence since they will notice your attention in their words.

Don't interrupt unless you have doubts

If you want to be a good listener, then listen. It seems simple, but for many people it is impossible. The bug of the I-also-want-to-opinion gets the better of us and it is practically impossible to have a conversation without wanting to put in the spoonful and say "to me", "I believe" or "for me things are like this".

Not interrupting the flow of speech is a basic condition that will allow your interlocutor to fully present his or her idea. Otherwise, believing you heard it would be like pretending to have watched a movie after having turned it off a few minutes into it. Think again about the matter from the other point of view and remember what it feels like to be constantly interrupted. Since I'm sure you know how unpleasant it can be, I'll ask that every time you feel like interrupting someone, remember the frustration you've felt when they haven't let you speak and express your ideas fully.

When a person feels that someone gives them the space to expand by talking, they create a close bond and place their precious trust in the other, making communication flow harmoniously and, above all, generating some esteem and appreciation. Isn't that what you want?

To avoid interrupting you must work on self-control. Is every interruption your brain invites you to make really necessary? Think about this while you feel like interrupting, because your brain will undoubtedly display a wide range of topics and observations about the topic your interlocutor is presenting, so you will probably feel compelled to break its flow to introduce your part. Don't do it automatically. Think about whether each of these interruptions is relevant, because in addition to becoming an annoying and unempathetic person, it is likely that you will only be able to confirm that saying that it is better to remain silent and look stupid than to open your mouth and confirm it.

With this I do not mean that you are a mute interlocutor. No one wants to talk to a wall, the conversation is by default an act of exchange between two or more people and interruptions are sometimes necessary to redirect the meaning of the matter in case your interlocutor deviates from the topic he intended to discuss. Many people want to talk about their problems and in the course of the conversation they change the topic because certain memories arose that lead them to new and diverse topics that had nothing to do with their initial dilemmas.

The interruption is also essential if you are looking to investigate the matter further. Psychologists know a lot about this, as we are used to using active listening in our therapies and ask questions like "And how does this make you feel?" or "Could you tell me a little more about what your relationship with your mother was like?" Asking questions is a way to show genuine interest in others and is essential in conversations. Or don't you feel helpless when you meet a friend and he doesn't ask you anything about your life? Ask simple questions that do not interrupt the flow but guide it or clarify situations. People are fascinated by talking and we are even more fascinated by the interest of others in what we say, which is why questions are a good tool that will touch the ego of your interlocutor.

Eyes with eyes

Looking into each other's eyes is one of the basic conditions of a good conversation. It's not about holding your gaze constantly, but about making frequent eye contact with your interlocutor. We all know that someone who does not look at your face is not a trustworthy person, we do not need to study psychology, because our brain is designed to read faces and their gestures, if someone does not want to share it with us, the alarm goes off of distrust.

A popular culture commonplace says that the eyes are the window to the soul, could you have a sincere conversation with someone who doesn't want to expose their soul? Furthermore, by looking into a person's eyes you can know much more about what they think than what their words say.

The body also speaks

Control of your body says a lot about you. Not only when listening. As I will explain later, a magnetic person has control of his posture and with it he communicates hundreds of things, among which is interest in a conversation. It's not just about looking at your interlocutor. Your body should be facing the other person, leaning slightly forward, with a look of genuine interest on your face. If you are in a place where other things are happening - a cafe, for example - you have to be able to concentrate on your interlocutor. We have all experienced situations in which we feel that we are speaking with an absent body, with a person who is watching what is happening behind us and we can even notice how their eyes follow the path of a situation that has nothing to do with our words.

The body speaks even if we don't want to and it can say much more than what we express. If you feel uncomfortable, you usually cross your legs and arms, or move an object with your hands. This, of course, will be interpreted by your interlocutor as a lack of interest in their words.

7 Don't be servile

There is a huge difference between a helpful person and a servile one. Unfortunately, some people often confuse things, mistakenly believing that by being docile they will be accepted by others. This is not like this. We tend to lose respect for people who don't respect themselves, and if we act in good faith, we will cast them aside. However, there will be others who take advantage of this submission to their advantage. A vitamin person knows perfectly well the difference between helpful and servile and would never fall into the latter, because their self-esteem prevents it. That's why we like them: they tend to help others by making their limits very clear. They know their worth and that is why they will not let anyone pass over them.

Submissive people have a sad disadvantage compared to the rest of us: they are capable of abandoning their dreams to satisfy others. Unfortunately for them, they believe that canceling themselves as people will bring them positive results, because by voluntarily submitting to the authority of those around them they believe they are avoiding a conflict.

If we talk about someone who is helpful, we are referring to a person who is willing to help others, who is, in some way, "at their service." This is a highly appreciated characteristic in social relationships, since part of humanity's success as an animal species has been precisely its ability to associate and achieve great things. We are helpful when we do a task, whether it is our responsibility or not, voluntarily and effectively to help a person. It is, in a few words, being a good person helping from the heart and in a selfless way.

In contrast, one of the deepest dangers of the servile character is that it engages in self-harm. A person who allows himself to abandon his dreams to obey the designs of another person - often in favor of the latter's objectives - is falling several steps in his self-esteem and this will make him a victim of unscrupulous manipulators. Servility is disastrous because it takes away our valuable time and degrades us as people, leaving consequences that can accompany us for many years.

Where is the border? One of the warning signs that we can identify usually appears if we doubt the appropriateness of doing a favor. If we are not sure about doing it, if we consider that perhaps there is something that does not quite fit us, it is because we do not really consider it a favor. If we doubt, we should reconsider the idea of doing what is in question. True favors, the acts that we do in a helpful manner, do not usually generate that doubt in us because we will never be helpful out of obligation. It is a contradiction in terms, since nothing we do under compulsion can have a healthy nature. If something transgresses our essence, it does not come from a good place.

I'll give you a very simple tool to figure things out. If you answer affirmatively to the question: If it were possible not to do it, would you do it? then it is most likely a situation where you play a menial role.

This does not mean that we should limit our helpful spirit because a context may suggest submission. This is frequently seen in work environments where our colleagues can reproach us for doing a little more than our share, as if it were a servile attitude. If we do it because we are proactive, great. If we do it to score points, we are making a serious mistake: entering into a role of servility can be disastrous for our aspirations, since people tend not to appreciate servile subjects, on the contrary, they have a negative evaluation of them, because servility is a synonym for low self-esteem. And it is very difficult for us to have appreciation for a person who does not have appreciation.

What are submissive people like?

I would like to address some of the main characteristics of servile and submissive people. Although both concepts are not exactly synonymous, generally a person who has one of these traits also has the other.

- They do not want conflicts: Submissive people usually avoid conflicts at all costs. In order to remain in an area of supposed peace, they can betray their feelings and ideas to agree with another person. Sadly, they often believe that their opinion is not worth enough to defend it in front of another. Likewise, they end up accepting a series of tasks and favors that they do not want to do, because they think that doing them will be easier than facing the conflict of saying no.

- They are shy: A person who usually represses what they feel and think is, generally, a person who develops an introverted and shy personality. This does not mean that all submissives are shy, but we can see a trait of shyness in some of the people with submissive traits. They often become the mute squire of a "leader" who speaks for them.

- They are negative: Submission and servility imply giving in to a series of personal dreams and desires to live in service of the dreams and desires of other people. Someone who lives with that heavy burden generates a negative personality, because they live in frustration.

- They are emotionally dependent: Submissive personalities are afraid. Afraid to speak, afraid to act, afraid to stand up for themselves. For this reason, they tend to generate relationships of dependency with people of a manipulative and authoritarian nature to whom they give their voice. This generates an emotional dependency that often translates into relationships of abuse and mistreatment.

-They are pleasers: These types of people constantly want to please everyone. They may do things they would never do on their own to keep someone else happy.

-They have low self-esteem: Submissive people explain themselves from this point: their behavior usually comes from low self-esteem, which is why they do not have confidence and security in themselves and allow others to take charge of their lives.

-They lack their own voice: A servile and submissive person does not have their own voice and if they do, they do not use it. Thus, they allow other people to impose their will over theirs and conform to other people's wishes.

As you will see, the traits of the submissive and servile personality are a sum of negativity in which the lack of self-love and security stands out, resulting in a kind of surrender to living life in the first person, delegating this responsibility to a "guardian." ", which is often nothing more than a manipulative person who takes advantage of their weakness. It is clear that no one fervently desires to be submissive and few people are willing to accept this condition even when they have the evidence before their eyes. However, some experiences throughout our lives can condition our character, leading us to accept a series of situations that someone with a healthy self-esteem would never let go. The logical question is, can a character of this nature be reversed? Yes of course.

Rebel recipes

Psychology has several tools to work on the submissive and servile personality that are mostly based on strengthening people's confidence. That is where the problem lies and where we must focus all our energy, because by now it will be clear to everyone that if you want to become a vitamin person, the last thing you want is to fall into attitudes of submission or servility.

One of the ways to work on your confidence is to take more responsibility and understand that there is no one in the universe who can take charge of your life except you. You are responsible for yourself and you must stand up. Have you ever thought that this sacred moment will never be repeated again? Don't let any more time pass, get up and walk. You have to stop delegating the important decisions in your life. The next time you have to make a decision, look inside yourself and follow your instincts. The worst thing that can happen is making a mistake, but you will have trained your confidence. The mistakes are solved and the lesson remains.

You must accept that not everyone will like you. And that's very good. The idea of seeking acceptance and affection from servility and submission is an aggression that you do to yourself and that will never be able to give you love, much less the respect of others. If you think that by being accommodating you will make people like you, you are making a serious mistake: follow your instincts and first look for your own acceptance. We'll see if it's necessary to have the others. I assure you that when you love yourself, you will see that the acceptance of others will seem overrated.

1.- You have to say no

Every time you feel the desire to oppose something, say it. Every time someone asks you for a favor that you don't want to do, don't do it. People greatly value those who have the courage to set their boundaries clearly and say no when they don't want to say anything else. Don't accept what you don't want. If the people who were around you disappear out of interest in your favors, so much the better: you don't need them and you will realize that they were only there for convenience. You are not here to receive crumbs of affection in exchange for favors. You are worth a lot and being complacent is a way of canceling yourself out.

2.- You have to talk

Take out your voice. You surely have a lot to say. As much as all human beings on the planet. But only by practicing will you be able to get it out. Then it's time to talk and state your vision of the world. Don't keep things to yourself. When you are at a social gathering and feel like you have something to add, do it. Don't talk for the sake of talking, of course, although at first practice won't hurt you. Don't be afraid to express yourself. After all, everyone does it. Your opinion is neither right nor wrong, it is just a way of seeing things, but if you present it in public you will begin to consolidate your confidence.

At first, even your voice may seem strange to you. If you are not used to public speaking, practice will help you. Try to have a good tone and volume, seek to convey security and you will see how little by little this becomes a reality.

3.- Don't feel guilty

The process of breaking with our former submissive and complacent self can produce feelings of guilt. How could I stop helping that person I've helped for so long? No. Don't feel guilty. Help is something that is given voluntarily and if you don't feel like doing it, don't do it. There will be no shortage of manipulative people who, faced with the prospect of losing your servility, will try to arouse your guilt when you abandon them. This will only confirm to you that they are bad people because if they really wanted the best for you, they would have helped you stop being subservient a long time ago. Try to find the origin of the guilt and reformulate your feelings. You may only feel guilt because you are used to acting for the benefit of others and to the detriment of yourself.

4.- Run away from toxic people

This, of course, is advice in all situations. However, it takes on greater importance when we want to combat a submissive personality, since toxic, abusive and manipulative people seek to take advantage of the servile character to take advantage. Then you must identify these types of people in your environment and cut the link immediately. I know that we have created bonds of emotional dependency and that it is not easy to break relationships overnight, but open the door and expel them from your life. We are talking about a question of survival. These people may not cancel you physically, but they do as a person. It's like they kill you every day. Don't let this continue to happen. The beginning will be conflictive, but it is much better to go alone than in bad company.

This liberation exercise will also help you strengthen your self-esteem and confidence. To the extent that you empower yourself, you will regain control of your life and everything will be like a snowball that gets bigger as the days go by.

5.- Be positive

Practicing positivity is an excellent way for you to shed the cloak of submission and take charge of your life. Because part of the responsibility of that servility is linked to negative thinking, as I explained to you a little further back. If we live with a heavy negative load, we are much more likely to generate a docile and easy-to-manipulate character. Optimism is a very powerful weapon to empower ourselves and take charge of our lives and our decisions.

The value of pride

I would like to close this chapter by talking a little about the value of pride for people. Pride is often associated with a negative character and arrogance. This is like many things in life: it depends on the use and how it is used. If we talk about positive pride, it is likely that we are talking about self-esteem, the value that a person gives to themselves. Remember: the love you give yourself is what teaches others to love you. It is very difficult for someone who is not good company for themselves to be good company for others.

Pride is not necessarily bad. On the contrary. Balanced and honest pride, based on positive values and self-respect, is the basis of healthy social relationships. This is why people-pleasers often have trouble having good relationships. If they don't appreciate themselves, how do they expect others to?

But if pride turns into arrogance, we become despicable and laughable beings: it is curious but arrogant people do not realize that their attitude can only deceive a few and that the rest of us find it pathetically amusing to see how they can believe yourself to be the center of the universe. A person who believes himself superior to others is unable to see his mistakes, therefore he cannot correct them or learn from them.

This is why I always invite my patients to cultivate what I like to call "Humble Pride." Love yourself without losing respect for others, without taking your feet off the ground and always keep in mind that the experience of living is much more pleasant if it is experienced with a kind smile on your face.

8 Our daily optimism

I met my great friend Francois during my first trip to Europe. I was twenty years old and had a burning desire to travel the world and expand the frontiers of my knowledge. It seemed to me that one of the best ways to begin this adventure would be in Spain, a country that at that time seemed exotic to me and made me think of Ernest Hemingway's books. The paraphernalia of bullfighting and flamenco, tapas and wine and all those postcards of paradisiacal beaches bathed by an incandescent and eternal sun prompted me to take a direct flight to Madrid. The city, in the heart of the country, did not have the sun I wanted. It was a beautiful city, full of people and taverns with delicious ham and exquisite wines, but I still needed flamenco and the beach. My ignorance as a young American had made me ignore the kilometers between the country's capital and its beaches on the Mediterranean. A little dazed, I checked into a hostel near the central Puerta del Sol, deciding to leave the next day heading south, a land of sun, sea and paella. Ole!

At the reception, an elderly man assisted me in very limited English. I couldn't blame him, after all my Spanish didn't go much further than "Buenos dias" and "Gracias." While we were trying to understand each other through signs, a small blonde boy with deep green eyes appeared at the reception. He looked at us with a smile on his face and approached. "Manolo, what this man wants is a private room with a bathroom for tonight," he told the old man in perfect

Spanish. They exchanged words and he addressed me in English: "Manolo says you have to stay two nights, the room with a bathroom has that condition. He says that otherwise it won't work for him." I reluctantly agreed as the price was a bargain and I wanted to take a bath. The boy stretched out his hand to me and told me with a French accent: "I am Francois, a lifer and a traveler." He put a smile on his face, I imagine it was due to my reaction to his particular presentation. "I'm Bill, an aspiring psychologist and…" I tried to imitate his grace but I couldn't find enough nerve to emulate his "trades." "Would you like a drink, Bill?" he asked me and I accepted without hesitation. Eighteen hours had passed since I left my house, and I wanted to sit quietly, have a drink, and contemplate my possibilities in the old world. I left my things in the room and we went out to explore the streets of a Madrid that was frozen in time. Francois seemed to know the city by heart and led me through small alleys until we reached a century-old tavern in the Plaza de Chueca where he ordered two vermouths. We settled at a table next to some old wine barrels and he said: "Spain is a wonderful place. Well, actually the world is a spectacular place if you want to see it that way." Shortly after speaking I noticed that his company was sweet and had the ability to turn my travel disappointment into urgent hope. Everything could be beautiful if you wanted it to be. "Look Bill, life is full of problems and pain. But these are not going to change no matter how much you think about them all day. You need to put them aside when you are not doing something to solve them. Otherwise they are going to persecute you and ruin your soul and spoil your appetite," he said with a laugh. Francois had the ability to act from hope, he seemed guided by a secret joy that he liked to exhibit because he knew that whoever gives a smile receives another in return. After a week I was still in Madrid enjoying his company. We toured the city from end to end but what I truly got to know was its optimistic spirit. This man had the ability to look to the future with an infectious faith that made good things happen. One morning we left for Toledo, a beautiful medieval city. Upon arriving at the station, we realized that we had missed our train. I regretted not having walked faster along the way, but Francois encouraged me: "Don't worry, sometimes things happen for a reason, we'll find a way to get there." He invited me to have a wine at the station bar. I took a seat and he headed to the bar. I saw him talking animatedly to a man and then he came up to me with two glasses and a smile: "Have you ever served as a machinist's helper?" he asked. It was clear that not. I was a psychology student on vacation in Europe. "Well, it's time to learn. Hurry up the wine because we will go to Toledo helping this man on a freight train," he told me and took a long drink to finish his glass.

His life was full of episodes like this. Francois knew that facing everyday life with a smile and good disposition led him to live all kinds of adventures, mostly positive. "Has nothing bad ever happened to you?" I asked him during our second meeting, years later in a bar in Naples where we had made an appointment by letter. "Of course, bad things happen, but many people think they happen more often than they really do," he replied. According to him, it is impossible to avoid misfortunes, but we can control thinking about them as something imminent. "That's why we have to live with optimism, Bill." His phrase has stuck in my mind and every time I feel like I am getting carried away by negative thoughts I think: what would Francois do? Today, in case you are wondering, my dear Francois has a grape farm in the south of France where he produces an exquisite Malbec wine that is sold at a very good price in organic supermarkets in the Occitanie region.

Optimism is a gift that nice people often share. It is a beautiful filter to see life with the hope that the best will happen and, if that is not the case, the negative will at least leave us a lesson from which we can draw something.

The perception of reality has direct consequences on our state of mind. That is why it is important to think about our predisposition for this perception. If we have a mental attitude that trusts in success and has hope that things will turn out well, we have already taken a first step. Living without optimism is closing the door before knocking. Optimism helps us to be aware of the miracle of existence and the preciousness of time, since it is no use facing life believing that everything will go wrong. Someone who starts a project believing it will fail is already lost.

Researcher Shawn Achor from Harvard University pointed out in his book The Happiness Advantage that it is possible to train optimism and change our outlook on life, thus managing to raise our levels of happiness. According to him, happiness is not a consequence, it is a cause. People do not achieve goals to be happy, he says, but rather we are happy and thanks to that we achieve our goals. This is why it is essential to reverse the paradigm and stop thinking about happiness as a goal. According to him, thanks to optimism, social support and resilience we can be successful at work since these are much more important than a person's intelligence.

The researcher carried out work in more than 45 countries and the results are astonishing. It is estimated that a positive brain can be 31% more productive than a brain with negative, neutral or pressure thoughts. According to their study, a salesperson's positivity translates into 37% higher performance than someone who does not have this feeling. If we talk about a doctor, the study indicates that they can be 19% faster, more precise and correct in their diagnoses if they act with optimism.

The good news is that optimism can be trained. Happiness has advantages and we can go out and look for them through a series of exercises.

1. The fervent desire

According to Achor, one of the parts we enjoy most about an activity is the anticipation. The desire for a thing can be even more pleasant than the thing itself, because we dream about it and the possibility of it existing makes our hearts race like the prospect of our birthday might have done during childhood. According to studies, mentally anticipating a pleasurable activity immediately increases our endorphin levels. This, as I have explained in other fragments, is because our brain does not usually make differences between reality and fantasy in chemical terms. This fact opens a window of opportunity: if we set an event that we fervently desire, every time we think about it we will have a hit of endorphins that will increase our optimism.

2.- Consciousness

Let's play mindfulness. Being aware of the present puts our foot on the ground and helps us keep in mind that we are a miracle, the product of billions of coincidences. We are here and now, why not celebrate it with optimism? Be aware of your body and your thoughts. They are yours, they belong to you, do not let them go uncontrolled through the meadow of pessimism.

3.- Thank you

Gratitude has a long list of positive benefits for people's physical and mental health. At the same time it is one of the ways to train optimism. Being grateful for everything we have, for the blessing of a new day, allows us to be more optimistic about the future.

4.- Meditate

Meditation makes the prefrontal cortex of our brain grow. Guess what. It is there where the emotion we call happiness is mostly produced. Regular meditation can help rewire the connections in our brain to increase happiness levels, reduce stress, and even strengthen our immune system.

In 2011, research from Harvard University established that with eight weeks of daily meditation an increase in the density of the gray matter of the hippocampus can be established. You don't have to meditate for hours, try to start with short sessions.

5.- Record your positive emotions

Human beings easily forget the good things that happen to us. Sometimes, we are so accustomed to the miracle of life that we let things pass without noticing the beauty in them. We believe that our lives run between boredom and routine, numbed to the point where we have no eyes to see the wonder. I invite you to write down something positive that happened to you throughout the day every night. As you progress with what we can call an optimism journal, you will see that there are many good things happening and that being aware of them will help you enjoy life from an optimistic stance.

6.- Sport is joy

I'm not saying this, the entire scientific community is saying it. If you are looking for information on how to lead a better life in any area, physical exercise will always appear as an unavoidable recommendation. Sport reduces stress, reduces symptoms of depression and anxiety, improves your self-esteem and helps you sleep better. Is there any doubt why it is good?

If you don't have experience or good physical condition, you can start with small acts, such as walking a little before taking public transportation or taking the stairs instead of the elevator. Little by little you will see how practice allows you to extend your limits.

7.- The owner of your thoughts

One of the characteristics of optimistic people is control over their thoughts. This makes sense: if you decide what you're going to think, the ghost of depressive or negative thoughts is less likely to creep into your head. If you want to live life with optimism and become a magnetic person, control your thoughts and every time you feel your mind leaning towards the negative, identify it as if it were a flock of migratory birds passing in front of you (yes, again). Look at them and tell them you don't want them, change them for more productive ideas. Daily training and meditation will help you do this.

8.- Accept responsibility

Optimism involves challenges, one of them, perhaps the biggest, is assuming our responsibility for our own life. Nothing will be possible if we do not take the reins of our life and direct it towards the destination we desire. In this sense, optimism is an end and a means, since achieving goals helps us be happier and that happiness is the fuel that we often need to achieve our goals. How do we achieve it? Taking responsibility that we are in control. Everything that is beyond our control must be left out of our concerns. If we can't do anything, what's the point of worrying?

9 THE POWER OF CREATIVITY

Let's be honest: we all like to be around a person who has the ability to see things from a different angle and who can say things that would never have occurred to us. It is a logical question: if we surround ourselves with people who are too similar to us, the world will seem like one of those mirror labyrinths at popular fairs in which the image is repeated ad infinitum, distorting in each reflection. Creativity in itself is a form of inexhaustible attraction, since it makes the creative person a constant mystery that we want to decipher.

A few years ago a young man appeared in my office distressed by what he considered to be an extreme shyness that was beginning to isolate him from his colleagues at school. As we talked, this boy told me a series of projects and fantasies that pleasantly surprised me: his creativity was an inexhaustible source of ideas and his problem was really the fear of exposing them in public. At his age, all the boys behaved in the same way and anyone who deviated from social conventions was called a freak and separated from the rest for daring to violate the boundaries of what they considered normality. His situation seemed paradoxical to me: this boy was full of creative vital energy but he wanted to get rid of it because at fifteen years old this meant becoming a stranger to the pack and being separated. We talked about it for several weeks and I tried to warn him something important: going against his creativity would be a very serious mistake, because within a short time this supposed abnormality among his high school colleagues would be rewarded in multiple ways, including becoming an attractive human being. for everyone else. "Calm down, boy. I think the best thing I can recommend is to be patient. Many times one seeks approval from those who are not worth it. Insist on yourself," I told him in our last session. I noticed that my words were not enough for a boy torn between two worlds: his fantastic genius and his desire to fit in with a group.

A year later, I found him with his parents in the supermarket. We chatted briefly and he surprised me with a warm greeting followed by "Thank you, doctor." He explained to me that he tried to be patient, as I had recommended, and above all, he sought approval from the right people. Those who appreciated his creativity. He found his space in the world and at a young age he was beginning to create a small digital animation company with some colleagues. Today, this man handles a quarter of the animations made in studios in the United States and he is not yet thirty years old.

For some people, the problem is that they cannot wait even a second and try to silence that little inner voice that suggests new ways of doing things. The sense of belonging to a group seems much more important to them than innovating and this, unfortunately, is a brain trap. Our mind is designed to keep us out of problems and creativity and new paths are precisely the opposite. However, we adore those who dare to be creative and do things their own way.

Why am I not creative?

There are a couple of lies in this subtitle. Yes, I am, we are, you are and will be the creative beings of tomorrow. The issue is why don't we allow that creativity to be the norm of our behavior? The famous Spanish painter Pablo Picasso once said: "every child is an artist. The problem is how to maintain the artist when he grows." Well, the explanation is something that most human beings have experienced: the fear of not fitting into society forces us, like my patient, to look for ways to silence that curious artist within us, that child capable of have one idea after another. We mistakenly believe that if we give free rein to our craziest thoughts we will be judged and considered freaks, but I have a truth to tell you: absolutely everyone can be considered a freak when you meet them. Think about the most "normal" (take that word with a grain of salt) person you know, the one who seems the most conservative and withdrawn. Investigate his intimate life and you will be surprised by the universe that may be there.

But fear is not limited to the fear of not fitting in. We often feel afraid of the judgment of others and of not being liked by everyone. There are those who mistakenly believe that being creative means being liked by everyone and this is a contradiction. You will never be able to please everyone, whether you are creative or not, so that idea is absurd no matter how you look at it. Regarding the judgment of others, I think you need to open your eyes once and for all: you cannot afford to let the opinions of others determine who you are. This, for the simple reason that they will not have to live in your skin every day and if you give them this power you will be stopping living your own life to live under the parameters and beliefs of others. Are you willing to let other people's opinions, tastes, dreams and desires prevail over yours? I have a little reminder for you: beyond any religious belief, an irrefutable fact is that in your current form and consciousness you will only live once. Every second is precious and other people's opinions are nothing more than a hindrance that will take time away from your life. Don't let that fear take over you, holding back your true self. Creativity makes up an essential part of your identity. No one, among the almost eight billion human beings who inhabit the earth today, thinks like you. So the solution is to face the fear, put it on the table and see if that little thing can dominate something as big and powerful as your identity. Is it worth thinking about the opinions of others? Maybe a little, because you are not a sociopath, but not enough to let this condition your abilities to create and express yourself.

Another enemy of creativity is perfectionism. Considered a virtue by some people, it actually represents a hindrance to work, as it often serves as an excuse not to act since "it won't be how I imagine it." Better something imperfectly started than genius without starting. It doesn't matter if the final product doesn't match what you imagined it would be, if you don't start for fear of not being true to that perfection, you'll never get close to it. In most fields, perfection is the result of a process, the product of failure and error that involves trying over and over again. If you believe in perfection, you will limit your creativity because it is also part of a training process. Better something done than in fantasy.

Creating creativity

Those who believe that creativity is a gift that some people are born with are very wrong. Creativity, like many skills, can be trained and enhanced with some tools. Interestingly, creativity has a snowball effect: the more freedom you allow yourself to be creative, the more creativity you will have over time. Something you should keep in mind is that creativity is a lifestyle, a constant search that should not be associated with a specific job. If you want to look at it religiously, creativity is a doctrine that requires a change of mindset in which you allow yourself the freedom to think outside the box.

To do this, there are some practical recommendations.

1.- Always carry a notebook

I'm sure you've had great ideas and said: oh, I'm going to remember this and develop this when I get home and sit in front of the computer. After a while, you remember that you had a great idea, but you don't remember exactly what it was about and your great project has been swallowed up for eternity. This often happens to us when we have great dreams and we think "I must remember this to tell my partner." After a few minutes, those fantastic facts are accompanying our brilliant idea in the sky of oblivion. This is why I always carry a notebook with me, even when I go to sleep. Well, actually it's a special notebook that I keep next to my bed to record all my dreams. That's what I call it: the notebook of dreams. I have almost twenty years of dreams saved and every time I read it I can relive things that have crossed my mind when I was sleeping.

Writing things down helps us not only record them but also helps us develop ideas. A childhood friend is a professional writer and one of his work strategies is to write even when he has no idea what he wants to write. He says that when he writes some single words about what he sees through the window, his fingers continue writing and his head finds some path that leads him to ideas that are interesting to him and after a few minutes, he finds himself in front of a text of which You can extract several clean paragraphs. He doesn't usually delete anything, because he once explained to me that even bad ideas can be the seed of genius.

2.- Playing is not bad

Console games about killing Martians are not a great intellectual contribution and have managed to create a harsh prejudice against all games in general, however, a study from the University of Michigan has shown that mental games such as crossword puzzles, Sudoku or chess can help you develop your creativity because they constitute a constant challenge and encourage you to produce new ideas because they pose problems that can be solved with creativity.

3.- Try not to have the same days

Neurological studies have shown that one of the ways to produce new neural pathways is to do different things every day. This is as simple as taking a different route on our daily routes. New information stimulates the brain and makes you more creative. And if you look at it from a logical sense, there is no worse friend to creativity than routine.

Falling into mental routine is fatal for creativity. Neurologists recommend that we have very different days, this way we stimulate brain activity and creativity. Even if we want to see the matter from a practical field, doing different things will keep us alert and stimulated, constantly receiving new information that will feed our creativity. In the end, one of the ways to understand creativity is based precisely on doing different things. Tomorrow, on your way to work, try a different path, it may take a couple of extra minutes, but you will be rewarded with what may be the beginning of a new adventure.

4.- Steal

This is not criminal advice, this is an artist recommendation. And not just anyone: Picasso had a controversial phrase that said "Artists copy; "geniuses steal." This basically means that you take everything you can from the outside, either way, your interpretation will make it different. Often we talk about original things only because we do not know their origin. This was experienced during the first years of the internet. Many people were considered geniuses by their environment because they did things that were incredible when the truth is that they only had a good internet connection and a curious mind that made them discover thousands of contents that their astonished colleagues were unaware of. Don't be afraid to take ownership of what you like, on the contrary, take it and improve it.

Creativity is not about discovering a certain form before anyone else, it is about your way of interpreting the great themes that humanity has addressed since the origin of our civilization.

5.- New music

A source of inexhaustible stimuli is music. But a better source is the music you haven't heard, the one that surprises you, the one you can't predict and that teaches you something new at every turn. People often close down their music collection as they age. As I say this I can't help but think of my father, a man who closed his music box forever on December 31, 1969. Everything else seemed too loud or shallow to him. If you behave like him, you will be directly attacking your creative capacity.

6.- The moments of creativity

If you work in the art world or have a hobby related to any artistic field, you have probably noticed that creativity has moments of the day. Or rather: that the day has moments of creativity and that it is necessary that they find you working. In this, each person usually has their favorite time to create, but I personally recommend the first thing in the morning. After a good restful sleep, your head is lucid and fresh and ideas flow through it more freely.

Generally speaking, as the day progresses, fatigue accumulates, making it more difficult for you to do intense intellectual work. That is why I recommend using it in the first hours of the day, between 7 and 10 in the morning.

Something similar happens with non-creative work: according to a study carried out on Japanese workers and published by the BBC in London, the morning hours are the best to absorb stress, so it is recommended to start the work day by tackling the most difficult tasks. complicated.

7.- Sweet dreams

To continue in the corporate defense of mornings I am going to take a scientific fact: a study from the University of Michigan established in the mid-80s that restorative sleep - of more than seven hours - for an adult is one of the mechanisms of neuronal reactivation. That thing about not sleeping and spending sleepless nights is a meaningless romanticization. Resting is a way to develop creativity and maintain good neuronal health. When you sleep your stress level is reduced and your conscious mind embraces the subconscious, strengthening the connection between your ideas.

According to National Geographic magazine, in a recent study, subjects who took regular naps during REM sleep (the phase in which dreams are most intense) performed better on creativity-based syntactic problems. That is, deep or REM (rapid eye movement) sleep helped people combine their ideas in new ways.

8.- Log out

It is difficult for me to think of anyone among my acquaintances who does not work directly with a computer. If I look around a few times, I can find one and, surprise, it is my sister's son, who is a painter. Chance? I don't believe it.

We spend hours and hours sitting in front of a screen and many of these are spent endlessly browsing social networks designed to create feelings of frustration and inadequacy. Remember: social networks are designed so that something is missing and the time you spend on them is not only wasted, it is harmful.

I cannot deny that the Internet is a brilliant invention that revolutionized the way we communicate, the problem lies in the use we give it. Most use it as a mechanism to channel anxiety, automatically browsing the same sites over and over again.

There is no doubt that being connected to the Internet has great benefits for creatives, since you can research a topic, seek inspiration or entertain yourself. But it is also convenient to live in the offline world.

The most powerful sources of creativity tend to be in nature. It is scientifically proven that a walk can help you generate new neural connections. Turn off the computer, get up and take a walk.

9.- Sex of ideas

This concept was created by the thinker James Altucher and is basically about relating two ideas that have no relationship with each other. You have to look for connections between two concepts that apparently share nothing, but that in the long run can help you create new things. Some of this is used in creative writing workshops. Teachers usually ask their students to tell them ten subjects, ten verbs and ten predicates and then relate them randomly.

10.- Challenge yourself

As you have seen, one of the most important lessons to be a magnetic person, the famous vitamin person, is that you must get out of your comfort zone. There is nothing good about staying in a space of comfort that does not help you grow. If you want to look at the history of humanity's progress you will find great examples of challenges with incredible results. The only failure is not trying, we all know that. Only by challenging ourselves will we achieve goals. Because starvation only brings routine and repetition. Your brain and creativity improve when you challenge yourself.

10 Let's laugh for a while

I would like you to think for a second about the people you find incredibly attractive without entering into a sexual field, those with whom you want to spend your free time simply because with them life is an experience outside the known. Now that you have them in mind, it's probably a smile on your face. Or at least a hint of a smile. This happens because you associate them with the joy and happiness they bring you. And a good part of this is because they are funny people.

A few years ago, a study by the University of Vienna established the close link between humor, intelligence and the attraction we feel for some people. According to the analysis, people who constantly make us laugh give us a feeling of well-being and tranquility that makes us want to share our time with them, therefore, if you want to become a magnetic person, humor is a fundamental tool.

Although many people consider comedy to be a natural gift that some people are born with, this is not entirely true. It is a process that can be trained and is often associated with specific cultures. The humor of the Spanish is not the same as that of the Japanese, nor is the latter a society in which laughter prevails. But beyond cultural differences, there are certain steps that can help us be funnier.

What makes us laugh? A study by the Department of Anthropology at Brown University established that there are three fundamental things that make us laugh: feeling superior to another who seems "less skilled" than us; the difference between what we expect to happen and what actually happens; or the release of anxiety. This, of course, is quite broad and generic, but it provides a good starting point to be clear about the origin of laughter.

I would like to rescue the work of behavioral researcher Vanessa Van

Edwards, who studied the topic and analyzed the work of several famous comedians to find the best tricks to improve one's sense of humor.

The unexpected

According to Van Edwards, the unexpected response is a short path to humor because it surprises. If someone asks you a question for which the answer is only yes or no, answering "shoe" will make that person look off initially, even if you later give them the answer they expected, it will have worked to make them laugh. This, however, only works if what is expected is concrete, because if there is room for ambiguity, "shoe" may not be funny.

The protagonist's turn

This is a classic and I have personally used it frequently. It's about changing the supposed protagonist of a conversation. I will give an example so that it is better understood: a few days ago I was talking to my sister on the phone when I heard my four-year-old nephew Mattias playing in the background. I then told him: "I see that you are with the child" and he said yes. Then I added: "And with Mattias too," implying that the "boy" was her husband. This trick always works and if you search on the internet for interviews with famous comedians you will find it among their main recommendations.

Anecdotes as a path

Being funny doesn't mean that you have to have a long repertoire of jokes or that every now and then you have to tell a joke to your audience. Being funny has more to do with what happens around us and knowing how to find the funny side. A common way to do this is to use our experiences and experiences with a humorous sense. Great comedians also do this with the phrase "when I came here…" as a filler to start telling an anecdote. When telling your stories, exaggerate wildly to the point that it is obvious that you are exaggerating and not lying.

Telling an anecdote also has the advantage that you master the story and you will not be nervous when telling it, because you know exactly what happened.

That it is funny?

Not all people laugh at the same things, but there is a certain convention about what is supposed to be funny. In this sense, a strategy to be funny is to think about what we ourselves find funny. Beyond social conventions and cultural learning, mirror neurons play a fundamental role in collective laughter. Because it is clear that the beginning of the path to being funnier is that what you say is funny to you. Mirror neurons are so-called "empathy cells" and they make us share the emotions of others. Haven't you noticed how contagious the mood of those around you is? If you spend the day with someone who is bitter, it is likely that after a while you will also feel bitter and the same thing happens with people who laugh, they usually infect our mood and will not make us laugh. This explains, for example, why comedy shows use the sound of recorded laughter when the script has a joke. What's more, with these laughs sometimes people end up laughing even when they don't find the joke in question very funny.

What is good humor for?

This question seems obvious, since most human beings know how pleasant it is to live in a good mood, even if not all of us achieve it. However, for those who are skeptical of smiles, for those who doubt the power of laughter, I want to talk a little about the benefits of living with a good sense of humor.

I'm not going to waste time reminding you of the type of society we live in. You know it perfectly and you will also know that you do not have great tools to modify it. If so, you only have one option left: face bad weather. A good mood will help you reduce your levels of cortisol, known as the stress hormone.

A study from Stanford University in the United States showed that laughter and good humor improve brain health and strengthen the immune system, as well as increase productivity at work.

According to research, laughing exercises different regions of the brain, especially in the amygdala and thalamus area.

Memory, attention and learning are also benefited by laughter: by reducing the production of cortisol, it increases people's ability to concentrate.

On the other hand, there are the famous endorphins, endogenous substances in the brain that generate the sensation of pleasure. Thus, laughing will give us a feeling of general well-being that could even contribute to palliative pain therapies. That Patch Adams thing wasn't just a Hollywood plot.

The process of laughter also increases the production of oxytocin, known colloquially as the "love hormone." Thus, when we laugh we are generating chemicals that appear in activities such as sex, exercise or meditation. In clinical psychology it has been shown that oxytocin boosts our confidence and self-esteem.

Humor plays a fundamental role in attraction. Being a generator of endorphins and serotonin, the desired neurochemicals of well-being, humor becomes a factor of desire for people: if a person makes others laugh, it is likely that in a short time they will become an object of desire .

11 The beautiful details

The most powerful people I have met throughout my life shared a higher value that I would like to share with you. All of them had the beautiful ability to live their personal relationships from the world of details. I will remember a great friend, Dr. Phill Donaway. This man had the ability to remember all the events that were relevant in my life and I believe that his great memory is largely responsible for us having decades of a solid friendship. I met him during my years as a student and we coincided in an elective course on classical philosophy. Nothing closely related to our careers but that was part of a taste for ancient Greece that we both shared. At that time, Katty, my wife, was pregnant with our first daughter and I didn't go to many of the parties that were held at the college. My responsibility as a boyfriend and future father prompted me to stay in the small apartment we shared, reading a book or simply talking with Katty. The day my daughter was born, Phill was the first person to call me on the phone and ask, "How has everything been? How are Katty and your daughter?" After exchanging a couple of words he asked me if it was appropriate for me to visit the hospital. We agreed that it would be better for me to come the next day, so my partner could rest. Sure enough, the next day he appeared at the hospital with a basket of clothes for my baby, a volume of Plato's Dialogues in a beautiful edition, and a small handmade notebook that he offered to Katty: they were the instructions for caring for a baby who had gathered since he found out we were going to be parents. I was amazed that a man in his early twenties had that level of commitment to our friendship. But life would give me hundreds of other examples of what being detailed is all about. We frequently talk about a topic that is interesting to us and a few weeks later I find a package in my office with a small note. It is about the book or some material related to our talk. Needless to say, this man has never forgotten a birthday in my family in over thirty years. Today this does not seem like a merit, since social networks like Facebook usually remind us that we should congratulate such a friend. But people of my generation will remember very well that until a few years ago only your close relatives remembered these kinds of things with certainty.

Detail-oriented people are nice people and we all want at least one of them in our lives. Whether as a couple or friend. The reason is very simple. When someone has a detail with you, whether remembering special dates for you or your tastes, it makes you feel important and loved. It makes you feel like someone in the world is thinking about you. And that is a very strong expression of empathy.

Before moving on to this point, I would like to remind you that the details do not equal the love and affection that a person may feel for you. The codes of expression of love are so many and so varied that we cannot measure the level of esteem we have for these attitudes. My father kept an immense love for my mother in his heart and that did not prevent him from forgetting some of her birthdays. I imagine you are thinking of someone the same. So don't be fooled: details are not a synonym for love, but we all love thoughtful people because they make us feel special.

Many people report losing their ability to communicate with others as they get older. And taking that care requires time and dedication and a clear mind. Multitasking focuses us on solving all kinds of daily problems, which in the end you don't solve either. Because we already know that the key to effectiveness is doing one thing at a time. But the rush, the multifunction, the work and the pace of life that we have keep us from being in the here and now, from focusing on "wasting" time thinking about the other, on dedicating a few words or carefully wrapping a gift. and pretty. Those details that, when you have responsibilities and are in a hurry, it seems like you can't invest the time to carry them out.

Some practical tips:

the power of the word

Look, this thing of being detail-oriented can be very simple if you are willing to open your heart. When was the last time you wrote your friends a nice word for no reason? What prevents you from doing it? We often live under the dictatorship of fear of ridicule. We believe that we should not do or say things because they might think badly of us. Forget it. Being thoughtful is about being yourself and saying what you think about the people you love. Send emails, or better yet, send letters. They don't have to be declarations of love, two words are enough for a person to feel loved.

The genuine interest

To be a retailer you must love people and show genuine interest in them. This means that you really care about them and that everything that happens to them will awaken your empathy. It's not about waiting for an illness or good news to make that call, it's simply about being interested in them, knowing how they are if some time has passed since the last time you talked to them. It's simple, but calling or writing to the people you love will make you thoughtful and lovable.

Save the dates

Nowadays, remembering a birthday has almost no merit. Social networks notify us so that we believe that we are accompanied, but what would happen if someone remembers the day your mother died and sends you a warm greeting? I'm sure you would think of that person with a smile on their face. There are many important dates for the people you love beyond their birthday. One of my dearest friends usually calls me every October 31 to tell me: "Hey, today we celebrate so many years of friendship, shall we celebrate?" Over time I have come to think that the day I don't receive that call it will be because something serious has happened. Try to make things seem natural, since it is not a work task and if your environment realizes that you do it as a merit to be remembered, it will seem a bit imposed.

Make different gifts

If you are one of those who gives away the fashion book, let me tell you that you are going down the boring path of the obvious. It's okay for your mother to give you underwear because it's useful and practical, but I'm sure you'll remember much more fondly the day she gave you something you didn't expect at all. For this, you must think about what a person really likes. It is not about what is obviously associated with him, like a book if he is a journalist or a brush if he is a painter. There are tastes that go beyond, for that you must know people.

It's not about expensive gifts, it's about making them meaningful. A few years ago I read a story about a company that instead of giving away pens with its brand and logo, gave away pens with each client's name.

Gratitude

If you want to be remembered in a bad way, act in an interested and ungrateful way. It is likely that throughout your life you have encountered someone like this. In my youth I met a boy with whom I thought I had developed a beautiful friendship. Sadly, I soon realized that he only wanted to benefit from the few things my family had and when he met other people with more money, he stopped looking for me and never appreciated the things we did for him.

Giving thanks is a spiritual exercise. It has been scientifically proven to lower blood pressure, strengthen your immune system, and make you an optimistic and happy person. Being grateful to those who have helped you will also make you a positive being with good social relationships. And, without a doubt, it will make you loved.

12 The sense of justice

I do not want to enter into the philosophical debate about what justice means, we all share a common base on the concept of justice that I am going to summarize as a moral value that drives us to act with the truth as a co-pilot and giving each being what they deserve. belongs and corresponds. For some it is a democratic value and is undoubtedly linked to the concept of the common good. Simply put, being fair is acting correctly, treating everyone as you would expect to be treated. This, of course, includes the treatment that someone should receive when they commit a mistake. Because being fair is recognizing our mistakes and accepting their consequences.

This is why being a fair person is not easy. Every day we commit injustices, many of them without realizing it, and we hurt our environment. The writer Victor Hugo already said it: "Being good is easy; The difficult thing is to be fair." Because life is full of injustices. Just walk through the streets of any city. We see poverty in the midst of absurd wealth, we see hunger in the face of food waste. As a fact: humans waste 48% of the food we produce.

Learning to act fairly is a fundamental value in a vitamin person. This is because it means that you can trust her and her judgment, even when her verdict is not favorable to you. You will always know that a just being acts with truth and equanimity. It is not about dividing things absurdly as in the anecdote of King Solomon, who tells that two mothers appeared before him with two children. One of them, dead. Both fought lively, declaring themselves their legitimate mother. The king ordered that they divide the living child in two and give half to each. The real one, moved, renounced him.

Justice is a sense of correspondence and therefore we must try to get closer to it, even when it affects us. A trivial situation usually occurs at family meals. When it comes to sharing dinner, there are often conflicts over the size of the dessert portions. It sounds irrelevant, but it can be a reflection of a personality. Someone with a sense of justice will choose the smallest in the hope that others will share a little of theirs and thus balance things. If by chance the largest portion comes before a righteous person, he will offer a part. This simple example can be taken to the work field and even to the sentimental field.

A question that humanity has been asking for thousands of years has to do with the fact that justice is a social interpretation or is unique for all social groups on the planet. Can we talk about how fair can be relative? It is important to understand that the sense of justice appeals to an assumption shared by all people. However, there are those who defend that there is a certain relativity in the concept, since each word is only an approximation of things. The phoneme "house" brings a different mental image for all human beings, even when everyone understands that it is a construction used to live. If we take this idea to court, we can play with the possibility that someone will defend their behavior as fair since that is how they understand this concept. But let's not fool ourselves, these juggles are precisely the kind of attitudes of despicable people, since justice will always be careful of the other.

On the other hand, we have to accept the risk that comes with acting with a sense of justice. The basis of many relationships is reciprocity and there we can find a kinship with justice, but there is a fine line: you cannot stop being fair because a person was not fair to you. If you act this way, you will be basing your behavior on correspondence and not on justice, so you will have a different way of being with each person, depending on how they are with you. Thus, your behavior will be a mirror and will be conditioned by others, in some way you will be a slave. In this sense, you should not waste your time comparing what you do with what the other does because you will turn your relationships into an endless scale that will not allow you to fully enjoy the present and that, without a doubt, will generate constant discomfort. It is true that it is difficult to do justice to those who have offended us. That is why it is difficult to carry equanimity as a banner.

The German physicist Albert Einstein once said "What a sad time ours is, it is easier to disintegrate an atom than a prejudice." Have you wondered lately which of your prejudices is most ingrained? You probably haven't done it and, even more likely, you probably don't know it either. That's why it's a prejudice: you think you're right about an issue without putting it to the test. The father of a friend from school was extremely homophobic and did not stop speaking against the LGBT community at the slightest opportunity. The guy used the classic arguments without much substance regarding what was "natural" and morality and good customs. According to this man, homosexuals were "degenerates" who should be confined in sanatoriums for not "behaving like good people" and having "disorders." I don't know if you, dear reader, share those absurd ideas regarding a community that has the right to be treated with equality and respect like any other. The fact is that my friend decided that he was fed up with his father and his prejudices and organized a dinner at his house to which he invited one of his coworkers who was homosexual. The dinner took place between wines and a wonderful atmosphere, the father laughed at every joke of his son's co-worker, a very nice man whom I met years later. When all the guests left, my friend's father told him that his co-worker was the nicest man he had met in a long time. "You should invite him more often, it's a delight to meet people like him," he told her. My friend was waiting for those words to apply the lesson and he didn't waste the opportunity. She told her father that maybe she would invite him and her boyfriend, an equally nice guy, to the next dinner. His father's face showed surprise and he corrected him: "his girlfriend, you mean." "No, her boyfriend shares an apartment with a lawyer from Massachusetts." His father was shocked. I couldn't believe what I was hearing. He sat down again with a broken face and after a tense silence he said that he couldn't believe the situation. "But he's so nice…" he said, shaking his head, as if disappointed about something. "I guess I was an idiot," he concluded later. My friend told him that for the first time he couldn't contradict him. "I have always thought of homosexuals as sick and it turns out that the sick one is me," the man said. After a long conversation about prejudice, the man finally seemed to understand how absurd it is to have an idea about something from a distance. It is sad when the mist of others prevents us from seeing our own landscape. Prejudices are, in any case, the absurd exercise of believing that we know something because we have heard others give their opinion about it.

The injustice of the world

The sense of justice is obviously related to injustice. This is what I would like to talk about now. From our birth we are exposed to what we could consider an injustice: why was I born in a poor country and not in a rich one? Why doesn't my family own my neighbor's assets? We grow up with a sense of injustice because somehow we compare life situations and reach the widely known conclusion that "life is not fair." And that is an incontrovertible fact: why should a small deer die in the teeth of a lion? Why must a man travel ten kilometers a day to fetch water for his family? Many questions that only have one answer: injustice. Now that the dish is served, that we know the conditions, does it make any sense to live immersed in this?

I would like to bring up the famous "Serenity Prayer", which is attributed to the American theologian and writer Reinhold Niebuhr:

> "Lord, grant me serenity to accept everything that I cannot change,
> courage to change what I am capable of changing
> and wisdom to understand the difference."

Living with a sense of injustice makes us uncomfortable beings. Besides being obvious, of course. Or do you think you are the only one who has noticed how unfair it is for a child to suffer from a horrible disease? I don't mean that you should accept reversible injustices, I'm just trying to explain that everything that we cannot change is background noise that we must accept as the context in which we have to live and is part of this wonderful experience. Let's call it "the rules of the game." These are things that you must accept and not live in constant complaint because that will only make you miserable. And a little unbearable, no doubt. Think about the people around you. You probably know someone who lives their life tormented by situations that they consider unfair and that they cannot change. I'm sure you don't appreciate this trait of his personality.

To address this, I recommend that when you feel this type of frustration you ask yourself the million dollar question: do I have any influence on what is bothering me? I can change it? If not, then fly pigeon, getting stuck in hopeless situations is a waste of time and energy.

Many times, the feeling of injustice is a product of comparison with other people. Some people often believe that the universe has not been fair to them by giving more resources to their neighbor. There is a little revelation for them: the universe doesn't care about them at all and the reasons that explain their neighbor's condition could be very different. All human beings are different, so comparing ourselves will only have a negative result. It's not about justice or injustice, it's about differences and understanding that what you see is just a part of others' lives. But above all it is about knowing that there is no point in living a life compared to others, since this means living a life other than others. Do you really want this for yourself?

It is often believed that the bad things that happen to us are a product of the injustices of life and in this I would like to remember a graffiti from my youth: "Things happen for a reason, because of a fool for example." Joke aside, it is important not to lose sight of the fact that we are the owners of our destiny and that feeling of injustice has to do with the fact that we do not like what has happened to us, but that feeling will not change things. The only thing that changes them is work, dedication and perseverance. To get up.

13 THE VALUE OF THE WORD

When I turned thirty, I received an extraordinary surprise. My great friend Julia, whom I met when we were five years old, showed up at my house after a long time without hearing from her. His presence was in itself a beautiful surprise, but things got much more interesting after the hugs and the questions about our lives. During dinner he asked me, "Well Bill, do you know why I'm here?" Of course, I assumed she knew: it was my birthday and after more than twelve years without seeing each other, my friend had decided to give me a pleasant surprise. "Of course, to share a bottle of wine with me and celebrate my birthday," I said, laughing. "You're sure? I think your memory is failing you a little. But I'm going to help you," she told me intriguingly and from her bag she took out an envelope that looked familiar to me. In childish handwriting, it was written on it: "Top Secret" and "Do not open." He handed it to me and said, "Well, now you'll see." The paper seemed worn, yellowish. Inside was a sheet of paper on which the same child's handwriting wrote as a title: "Contract of eternal friendship." The text then read: "I, Julia Isackson, declare that I will be a lifelong friend of Bill Waits, no matter what happens. With this contract I commit to celebrating together when I am old and turn 30 years old. And for this to be real, we both signed this document." Below this tender letter appeared two abstract scribbles that acted as signatures. I could not believe it. Without being able to contain it, two droplets appeared in my eyes and rolled down my cheeks. Of course, now he remembered: the tree house, the summers in the garden of his house where his father installed a small plastic pool for us, the mosquitoes and the ice cream... oh God, there were so many things together. Julia was a person of her word. A person who kept his promises and there he was, in front of me to prove it. Clearly, my affection for that woman was not born that day, but it did reinforce the reasons why we had become great friends. This is a person who will always have a magical correspondence between the things he says and the things he does. That is, without a doubt, magnetic.

Can commitment to the word be cultivated? Of course. It is true that there are people who have been acting in this way for many years, so today it is relatively easy for them to act consistently, but I assure you that it is never too late to start creating the habit of backing up our sayings with facts.

I'm not a particularly religious guy, but the Bible is a spectacular book. In my behavioral therapies I usually quote to my patients a passage from the Gospel according to Saint John in which it says: "In the beginning there was the Word, and the Word was with God, and the Word was God. He was in the beginning with God. Through him everything was made, and without him nothing was made that has been made. In him was life, and the life was the light of men". This fragment seems to me to be a beautiful reminder of the power of words at all levels: words build and destroy, words are the beginning of human life and our interpretation of the universe. Likewise, words are the beginning of a habit or a personality trait. Our inner speech is made of words that give meaning to our behavior. Therefore, the first step to strengthen our coherence is to perceive our words in another way. We must understand that a commitment or promise is unbreakable. It's not about a maybe, it's about a yes. If we understand the value of the pledged word, we will be faithful to it. To do this, commitments must be perceived as an inviolable contract.

One of the ways to make your perception of your commitments that of an impossible contract to break is to write them down in a notebook. If you keep a kind of "commitment diary" you will have a record of them and the very fact of writing them will make you interpret them as something sacred. It is proven that leaving something in writing makes our mind remember it more easily and consider it more important than everything we simply leave in our memory. Our brain works through codes and reinforcements, the symbolic plays a fundamental role in the interpretation we have of the universe, therefore, I recommend that you keep your commitment diary in a "sacred" place in your home. We all have corners where we keep our important documents, our passport, the deed to the house or our wedding photos. Well, that is where your commitment diary should be, I assure you that in this way you will begin to consider that what is written there is sacred and must be fulfilled as a contract.

Term

Commitments are meaningless without a time frame in which they must be carried out. It is useless to say that I am going to quit smoking if I do not sign this verbal contract in a time and period that makes sense to it. When am I going to stop smoking? Today, tomorrow, in a year, in a decade? When establishing a commitment you must set deadlines that give it meaning. But be careful, be realistic with the times. You can't say that you are going to lose ten kilos in a week nor that you are going to read a book a year. If you want the people around you to admire you for keeping your word, try to be relevant on deadlines. And of course, comply with them to the letter.

It is important that you think about the deadlines and dates regarding the commitments you make with your environment. If someone asks you to help them mow their lawn next Sunday, you should be clear that you will be able to do it. People often accept distant commitments because they find it difficult to say no or because in their best fantasies they believe that they will be willing to do it because it is a distant date, so they accept and then spend hours looking for excuses to try to avoid the commitment. To prevent this from happening to you, I recommend using an agenda in which you record important events and see if you can really comply or if it is just a desire to help more than a real will. The power of the pledged word lies precisely in that, in doing what you said you would do. Many times it is better to say that you cannot commit than to fail to commit. One of the simplest ways to know whether or not you should pledge your word is to think that what they ask of you should be done today. Would you help me paint my house? Would you lend me money? Could you come to my house? It is true, there is some room to differentiate whether this will be today or on a certain date, but it is good to know if you will be willing to do it today to know your true disposition.

The word is love

One of the ways to show people that you care and that you consider them in your heart is by keeping your word. It is very easy to throw statements into the wind, promise this life and the next and swear to heaven that we love a person. However, only the consistency of facts can truly demonstrate that love. A person of his word will have no problems confronting these types of statements with facts. And when you manage to establish coherence between the two things, you become a trustworthy person, a person that everyone wants to have around because they can simply trust you.

Fulfilling what is said is a way of showing respect towards others and that is precisely what most human beings seek. One of the big self-esteem problems that adults in the United States suffer from is related to a feeling of lack of respect. People believe that they deserve more respect than they receive and that one of the sources of this frustration is found precisely in their immediate environment. If you keep your word and honor your commitments, you will show others that you respect them and for the same reason you will become a magnetic person: everyone wants to surround themselves with people who treat them the way they believe they deserve. When someone asks you for a favor that may involve a commitment, try to take this action as an honor. That person does it because they believe they can trust you. And that, you will know in advance, is an honor that we cannot always refuse. Of course: a good reputation entails a dose of work, no one said it would be easy.

Learn to say no
The power of the word also lies in using it to know how to say no. There is a wide range of literature on how to learn to say no when we don't feel comfortable with a situation. However, opposing it is still very difficult for many people who end up accepting commitments that they did not want and that they often fail to fulfill, thus becoming unreliable beings simply because they did not know how to say no. I know that social pressure can be brutal and softens us into accepting compromises in a moment and that we often think: "well, I'll say yes, but then I'll find an excuse." And that is precisely the problem: it is infinitely easier for us to find excuses than to have the courage to be coherent and express what our hearts tell us. In the end, we look bad for not fulfilling something we did not want to fulfill. Thus, the obvious recommendation is to accept only those commitments that seem relevant to us and that we are really willing to fulfill. Your word is worth a lot, give it the place it deserves by learning to say no. I would like to dedicate a few words to a curious phenomenon that usually happens to all of us: in addition to having problems saying no, we usually look for arguments to support our refusal. We

believe that we must give an explanation every time we do not feel the desire to do something certain and we resort to a long list of lies or pretexts to support our desire. The next time you identify a situation of this nature, venture with a simple: "I'm very sorry, but I won't be able to." And period. You don't owe anything to anyone and unless it makes sense to you, you don't need to explain the reason for your will.

The clarity

A person of his word does not mess around. There is no "maybe". Things are simple: yes or no. If you are not sure if you can keep a commitment, just say no and if circumstances change, you can resume the conversation and say: "well, I don't know if it's a little late, but now I can." The ambiguities are more unbearable than the negative ones. Think about it regarding your environment. Surely you know a person who often says that he will "try" to accomplish something and you never know if that attempt will be true, if it is a way of discarding himself or if he will just really try. Ambiguities make you an untrustworthy person. And no matter how much love we may feel for them, these people are not our favorites for the simple fact that we don't know if they will be there when we need them.

Doubt and lack of clarity are also a sign of a weak character, who does not know what he wants and who is not mature enough to have things clear. This is a reflection of an unstable and unambitious personality, which in other words is an invitation to flee your company in the long term. Let's be honest: no one wants a partner or a friend who doesn't know what they want or doesn't have the courage to go get it.

14 Humility

The American writer Ernest Hemingway once said a phrase that stucked in my mind: "There is nothing noble in being superior to your neighbor; "True nobility is in being superior to your inner self." It is very simple and profound advice at the same time. In the times in which we live, the maelstrom of supposed productivity and the haste with which we are supposed to navigate the world have made us think that success consists of surpassing those around us. The false belief that we are in a competition with winners and losers has led many people to believe that humility is a burden they must get rid of, since arrogance automatically grants them the place in the world that they believe they deserve. Nothing more false. One of my favorite professional challenges is treating people with narcissistic traits, because if I can get them to approach their personality from another point of view, I think I have made a great contribution to the world: humility is a very powerful tool to propel our society towards a better future. better place.

I would like you to think for a moment about the contrast: isn't arrogance one of the most unpleasant attitudes you can find in a person? If you do a quick review, it should be in the top three of things that make a person dislike you, along with envy and rudeness.

Vitamin people are humble by nature. They know that they are not the center of the world and are willing to recognize their limitations and weaknesses and are open to learning. This is a fundamental factor of humility: recognizing our mistakes and having an open heart to assume habits and behaviors that allow us to be better people.

In some way, humility consists of forgetting our ego without forgetting ourselves, as some people mistakenly believe. If you have ever had contact with Buddhism, you will know a little about what I am talking about. The French Buddhist monk Mathieu Ricard once wrote that "a humble person has nothing to lose or gain. If they praise her, she thinks it is for what she is capable of achieving, not for herself as a person. If you are criticized, you think that exposing your faults is the best help anyone can give you." And Buddhism assures that the best teaching a person can receive is the one that shows them their own flaws.

What's the point of knowing a long list of things if we don't know how to see our hearts? Humility is closely related to the sense of justice that I spoke of a little above. You cannot be just without being humble, nor can you be humble without knowing what justice is. This is because justice and humility allow us to treat all people equally, having a genuine interest in them and their well-being. A humble person is a desired company because he listens honestly, is simple and understanding without leaving aside his character.

Can you learn to be humble? Yes of course. It is hard work but it is worth it, because it will help you be happy.

Do not judge

People are not worth the things they have, the country they were born in or the clothes they wear. People are valued for who they really are, for their values and their personality, for the ethics with which they live life. If you judge them based on material things, you are losing your sense of priorities and you need to correct the course of your life. When you stop judging you become a person open to knowing what truly matters and you become freer: judgments and prejudices are above all a burden for those who exercise them, they are the prison that does not allow them to leave an area in which they are not allowed. It is completely comfortable, because if you mistakenly believe things about the people around you, you will not be able to fully enjoy their company.

For this reason, one of the exercises to cultivate humility is to have equal treatment with all the people around us: one of the fundamental mantras to cultivate what I consider to be the gift of humility is to keep in mind that we are not superior. to others. Nor inferiors, that is of course. No person is worth more than another, it is a fundamental principle.

Be wrong

At the time of writing these lines, there are 7,753 million people on the planet and each of them has a vision of life. Do you think everyone is right? Do you think you are always right? Humility starts from doubt: it is not about believing that we are wrong in our vision of the world, it is about keeping in mind the possibility of being wrong and, therefore, being open to the possibility of accepting that mistake. One of the saddest things about pride is the fact of refusing to learn. People who believe they know everything and are always right are closing the door to knowledge. This is deeply sad, since there is no greater wisdom than constant learning and the confrontation of visions. I don't mean to say that you should always agree with others, but leave the door open. It will be useful to you in many ways. Not only will you be liked better, but it will allow you to look inside yourself to determine if your beliefs are the best. Remember that we have a long list of ideas that may not be true and that we only defend and respect them because we are inserted in a culture, in a family, in a society, in a group of people who share them. The fact that an idea is shared by thousands of people does not make it correct, it only makes it popular.

In that sense, it is important that you recognize that perhaps your judgments are wrong. That perhaps what you believed about a certain matter is wrong, that you made a mistake. Accepting our failures is a tremendous step on the path of humility, only an arrogant fool would try to hide his mistakes when the evidence shows him that they are mistakes. It is not bad to recognize them, on the contrary: it will only make us grow.

You are not the center of the world

It is likely that in an attempt to reinforce your self-esteem and personality, your parents have told you that you are worth a lot, a lot, and that you are very special. That is true, as it is also true that each human being is worth a lot, a lot, a lot. You are not the center of the world and that is fine. Free yourself from that weight, because it is false and does not bring you anything good. You are a person with your flaws and your virtues, recognize the former and learn new virtues, life is too short to believe that the universe revolves around you, the sooner you internalize it, the better for you. You will live free knowing that you are no better or worse, you are a very valuable human being, like everyone else. Knowing how to see your limitations is a window to learn to improve them.

Since you know that you are not the center of the universe, then you will be able to recognize the value of others: if you trust them, you will be able to experience their presence without prior judgments. This is a starting point that allows you to experience people from a blank page. Their behavior - and yours - will write that sheet and determine whether the trust you gave them has been reciprocated.

In the same sense, since you know that you are not the center of everything, you will be able to collaborate better with others, since you recognize that the group can do much more than the individual. This is a powerful tool for those in charge of groups of people. He who understands that individualism is not the path has already approached the goal.

One way to understand that you are not the center of the universe and that you care about others is to practice active listening that I already explained in a previous chapter. To summarize: simply talk less and listen more, it is one of the simplest and most profound forms of humility.

Humble but not submissive

One of the mistakes that people usually make in their attempt to cultivate humility has to do with the mistaken idea that they have to cancel themselves as people to always agree with others and thus be liked. This is not the case: submissive people are not liked because we consider that their weak character does not deserve our attention. This weakness represents a sad denial of them as people and turns humility into servility. Beyond occasional instrumentalization, no one wants to surround themselves with servile people, because their identity disappears and they become an echo chamber for the people around them. Humility is not about this: on the contrary, a humble person knows how to see the value of everyone else, including their own. To stoop to servility is to cease to exist as an autonomous entity. Learn from the humble, not the submissive.

Thank you

After some consultations, my patients often joke with me because some consider that I place too much importance on the value of gratitude. "Hey Bill, thank you very much," they tell me in a joking tone, appealing to an internal joke in which I ask them when was the last time they gave thanks from the heart for something that is not tangible. We live life as if it were something we deserve and not as a sacred gift. We have forgotten the profound value of being grateful for the possibility of being here, reading, writing, living, loving, dreaming.

Gratitude is a fundamental part of the gift of humility. It allows us to look into the eyes of how fortunate we are to be alive and to enjoy a long list of incredibly good things. Because if today you woke up with a kiss and received love, you are privileged. When we are willing to be grateful, we are accepting that we are not the center of the world and that what we have is the product of the actions of others and that has benefits in many fields, including your health. A study showed that the feeling of peace that gratitude produces helps lower your blood pressure and strengthen your immune system. It's not just about being in good spiritual shape, it also reflects on your body.

Vitamin people are grateful by nature and this is one of the reasons that makes us want to be close to them and do them favors: their gratitude will make us feel that it was worth shaking their hand and that it will even feel natural for us to help them: gratitude establishes strong links between people.

Generosity

Like gratitude, generosity is part of a chain of favors that makes up humility. If you are able to be generous with what you have, it means that you give higher value to people. For a humble person, nothing can be worth more than his neighbor, so sharing material goods is a living demonstration of that. On the other hand, think a little, what is the point of avoiding generosity? Do you really need everything you have? We live in the age of abundance and we are prisoners of the fear of scarcity. I know that we cannot always share absolutely everything we have, but if you reflect a little, it is not necessary to keep everything. Much less in developed countries. The culture of the fittest and every man for himself has created petty beings who avoid sharing at all costs. Generosity breaks that chain and turns you into a humble and kind being that everyone wants to have by their side.

Generosity can also be expressed in immaterial terms. People usually come to my office who are willing to share all their assets but not their feelings or their hearts. Memento Mori, remember that you will die, and it is of no use to you to live in the greed of feelings.

Ask for help

Humility is understanding that there are thousands of things that we do not know or cannot do. Ask for help. Don't hesitate to ask for help. Please ask for help if you need it because believing that you can take care of yourself is crazy that in the long run is related to self-destruction. It is common to see people who believe themselves to be self-sufficient, driven by pride, walk again and again towards error. Instead of appearing multifaceted and self-possessed, they only demonstrate what humanity has known for millennia: stubbornness only takes up your time and energy.

The guidance of other people will also help you establish strong bonds with others, since human beings like to feel that someone respects them and considers them useful and skilled in some field. Try it with a friend. Ask him for help with something you think he's very good at, and you'll see a spark of joyful pride appear on his face at the respect you show him. And this will undoubtedly strengthen your friendship. That is why it is important that when you ask for help and receive it, you show gratitude and admiration. Don't be flattery. Be honest and fair: When you have an opportunity, praise the help and qualities of the person who gives it to you.

15 Self-confidence

One of my best friends from college met a girl at a party. They exchanged
phone numbers and the next day he invited her to dinner. She was a little
hesitant but finally told him that she would meet him at an Arab restaurant in
the center of the city. My friend, Gene, called me to tell me very excited that
this beautiful blonde had agreed to go out with him. I congratulated him and
asked him to keep me posted. A few days later he called me to tell me about
the development of his appointment. She was a charming girl who worked as
a ghostwriter of political texts. He comes from the center of the country and
dinner ended with a walk around the city, a couple of furtive kisses and a
promise to see each other soon. Their relationship developed quickly and after
two months Gene called me to tell me the latest news. The girl was charming,
very intelligent and extremely cultured. However, he felt that within all those
attributes something was not quite right. "There is a situation that is
frequently repeated and that is that she never knows what she wants," he told
me, a little disappointed. "If I ask her what she wants for dinner she tells me
that I'd better choose, if I ask her if she wants to go to the movies, she tells
me that if it's okay with me, that's fine for her." This seemed minor compared
to the girl's qualities, but my friend was not convinced to continue with the
relationship. "It's not about trifles like choosing dinner, this is just the tip of
the iceberg," lamented Gene.

After a while, Gene asked me to have a few drinks and discuss the matter with me. "Bill, I think I'm going to leave her. The more I get to know her, the more I realize that her insecurity affects me too much." In his story, my friend said that the girl frequently talked about who her parents were and what friends they had and how much they had accomplished in their lives, trying to demonstrate value through other people's achievements. "It's as if he wanted to show me a catalog of great men who have been around him or his family and with that validate himself as a person," he noted. According to Gene, one of this woman's fundamental problems was trying to convey these insecurities to my friend. It was, he said, as if it wasn't enough for her to feel insecure, she wanted him to feel that way too. "Every day he tells me, 'We're so alike, Gene.'" And of course, every day they looked more alike because she blended in with him. He had begun to imitate my friend's tastes, completely abandoning the person he seemed to be before they met. On the other hand, this woman lived comparing herself to her sister, in an endless lament for what she considered the injustice of not being as intelligent or beautiful. "Well Gene, I think that as a psychologist you will know very well that you are dealing with an insecure person. Now it's your decision whether you want to continue with it or not, but you know what that means," I told him when he asked my opinion. After a few months, they separated. She was a very valuable woman, but I didn't know how to see it and that seemed like a very heavy burden for my friend. "Under other circumstances I would have kept going, but I'm not 20 years old anymore," he explained to me. I don't judge: no one should share their time with someone who doesn't fully satisfy them.

Insecurity is a very heavy personality trait for those around us. There is no single or static component of insecurity. There are those who suffer from it to a greater or lesser degree and it can vary over time. It can also be combated with behavioral therapy. And it is, without a doubt, a trait that a vitamin person wants to avoid.

Self-confidence implies being aware of our value. This is obvious but it is necessary to explain that we all have voices that make us doubt our talent and security implies knowing that these voices are almost never right. I'm not telling you that you should silence them, because we must be aware that we are worth a lot, but not more than other people. Self-confidence is not an excuse for arrogance and arrogance. What's more, we often discover that people with narcissistic traits are actually insecure and try to disguise this trait with a mask of superiority.

You are not superior, you are capable. And when you manage to internalize this feeling, when you manage to communicate it to yourself and understand it, you also communicate it to the outside. If you know that you can trust your talent and ability to carry out a task, you are communicating to the world not only that you will do it, but that it can trust you, because you yourself trust yourself.

The writer Oscar Wilde once said that loving yourself is the beginning of a lifelong romance and I would like to add that it is the healthiest and most necessary romance you can imagine. The trust we place in ourselves has a lot to do with our self-esteem, one of the fundamental bases of our emotional stability, since it involves the entire paradigm that we create around ourselves from our birth. In simple words, it is about loving everything you represent, but doing so in a fair and honest way, as true love is: without idealizing or hurting, trying to improve every day.

And precisely a good dose of self-confidence is the beginning to improve as people: if we believe in ourselves, in our abilities, we will be able to believe that they can be better every day. If you believe in yourself, it is very likely that you will make risky decisions that will help you become better because you will face each challenge with optimism.

According to the book Oxford Handbook of Positive Psychology, lacking confidence can be a heavy burden: "If the person lacks confidence, there will be no action. This is why lack of confidence is sometimes referred to as 'paralyzing doubt'. Sometimes doubt undermines effort before an action begins or while it is being carried out."

To return to the case of my friend and his ex-girlfriend, I would like to remember a scene that he told me on the phone: "This girl is so insecure about herself that she just received news about a job vacancy at the United Nations, since I met her, she told me about her dream of working there, but she doesn't want to apply because she thinks she won't get it... do you realize? If you don't apply, there's no way you'll be able to fulfill your dream one day," my friend lamented. Here's how things work: trusting yourself won't make you the best in a certain field or get your dream job, but it will make you take the right steps to achieve those goals.

Improve your self-confidence

We could talk for hours about the importance of self-confidence, but I think what you are really looking for in these lines is how to improve it. Because yes, it can be improved and cultivated.

Broadly speaking, the beginning of this process is related to a change in your beliefs. We talked about resetting the machine and filling it with new information. That computer that is your brain must be programmed again so that it uses the operating system in which you are worth much more than you think. Let's start with the affirmations: repeat with me: "I can, I can, I can." This is not magic, it is simply the beginning of what you must believe. "I am smart and I am capable of facing challenges." Because of course you're smart! You are reading a book to be smarter, it shows you that.

I'm sure you've received compliments on some of your skills in the past. Keep them in mind when facing a challenge. Remember that people have trusted you in the past, why wouldn't you in the present?

start moving

This is not a metaphor: start moving, because physical exercise is the beginning of everything. I don't have to explain to you the great benefits that doing an average of 150 minutes of exercise a week has for your body. The World Health Organization has said this countless times and we all know it because if it wasn't the WHO we heard it at school. According to the American Psychological Association, exercise improves our mood and is devastating against depression and anxiety. In medical terms, we must remember the role of endorphins as connectors of neurons in the nervous system, something like a connection between the body and the mind. They transmit pleasure, happiness, joy and help reduce pain. That is why when we exercise, these hormones are activated and improve mood, increase self-esteem and reduce anxiety and stress. Sport can help improve your confidence if it becomes a prolonged activity over time, as it requires a certain commitment and you can already consider the mere fact of getting up every morning to go to the gym an achievement. Furthermore, sustained sport will change your body for the better and that, although it sometimes pains us to admit it, is a boost for confidence.

Look for discomfort

The comfort zone is one of the great dangers for our personality. With the apparent calm of a safe place, it prevents us from growing permanently and leaves us stagnant in a space that often resembles mediocrity.

Personal safety is related to comfort in any space, so if you seek to leave the spaces in which you usually move, you will learn to be comfortable and confident in all spaces, expanding your comfort zone.

And what is the famous comfort zone? Well, it is simply the routine that you do every day and that you do not violate because "you are not like that." If you want to gain confidence in yourself, do things you don't usually do, like learning to dance or challenging yourself with small gestures like striking up a conversation with a stranger on public transportation. I invite you to think about one of the things that you never imagined yourself doing and that you dare to try it, you will see how this is a first step and helps you consolidate your confidence, because, among other things, it will show you that it is not so terrible coming out of the shell. Quite the opposite.

You are already safe

One of the most particular characteristics of our brain is not distinguishing between the veracity of thoughts, which is why you can feel sad when you start imagining the death of a loved one. So we are going to use this condition to our advantage. We are going to act as if we were people with a high degree of security and to do so we must make a series of determinations:

-Accept challenges and behave as if you were completely sure that you will be able to solve them without problems

-Walk straight and raise your chin slightly

-Greet with confidence

-Don't be afraid to ask questions

-Say no when you feel it

-Look people in the eyes

-Speak with a solid tone

Cultivate yourself

There is a proverb that says that a bird that perches on a branch of a tree is never afraid that this branch will break, because it trusts in its wings. Well, one way to have wings is to prepare for life. Constant learning is the basic tool for this: read books, take courses, listen to podcasts, watch documentaries. Never stop learning. Filling yourself with knowledge will make you fully trust your abilities, even more so if the cultural products you consume are linked to your work environment.

No problem

One of my favorite mantras for people who have shyness issues is to ask them to think about the world in 100 years. Do you think any of the decisions you make will matter? Even think of the world if you decide to ask a question in a college class. Do you think your classmates will be upset? Do you think they will remember it in a while? No nothing happens. Do what you feel, don't stop living because of the fear of your environment. Enjoy your life because every minute is invaluable. If you manage to internalize the idea that it is okay to break your shyness, you will discover that your confidence naturally increases, because you understand that the only thing that matters is that you live fully.

New image?

The feeling of personal security is linked to our physical perception. This is not about superficiality, I am talking about a study by the University of Valencia in adolescents that demonstrated the ineffable link. So, curiously, it is one of the aspects that we can easily modify. The perception you have of yourself is also linked to the clothes you wear, so if you change your style, your brain can also interpret that there is a change underway. Professor Adam D. Galinsky, of the Kellogg School of Management at Northwestern University, had a curious finding: according to his work, participants in a study who wore a white laboratory coat demonstrated greater concentration. This means that when their participants dressed as doctors, they behaved as if they were one.

Turn fear into challenge

Biologically, fear and excitement have the same origin: adrenaline. This means something very powerful. In theory, we can transform our fears into the driver of risky action. This was what Dr. Alion Brooks found in a study published in the Journal Experimental Psychology. There, Brooks divided a group of students into three and put them under pressure: they had to make a presentation before a jury. He didn't say anything to the first group, while he asked the other two to say "I'm calm" and "I'm excited," respectively. The results showed that the third group, which associated nerves with enthusiasm, performed better on the task, modifying their fear into courage.

This means that internal dialogue and changing perspective when faced with a task that could be associated with fear can change our performance.

Insist on you

One of the stories with which I began this book recalled the story of my schoolmate who was considered a "freak." His personality is a great example of how to insist on who you are and have enough security to understand that you are you and none of that background noise that is other people's opinions should make you change. I'm not telling you to close yourself off to constructive comments from your environment, I'm telling you to be yourself and feel comfortable with who you are. You have failures and errors, give them the importance they may have but do not block yourself from them and accept yourself as you are, within you there is enormous potential and it is based on maintaining your essence. It is normal to doubt ourselves, doubt is part of a healthy personality. Only fools are capable of remaining certain. But doubt cannot paralyze you. Take risks, insist on yourself.

One way to reinforce this idea is to keep your achievements always at hand. When you doubt, when you feel afraid for the person you are, remember all the good things you have accomplished throughout your life. I'm sure the list is long and remembering it will help allay fears and build your confidence.

16 AND YOU, HOW ARE YOU?

During my years as a university student I met a person who everyone called Yoyo. It took me very little time to understand the origin of this nickname, based in "Yo" the Spanish word for Me, when we met at a social gathering and the man spent more than an hour explaining how he was the best at each of the topics we covered, from surfing to cooking Neapolitan pasta. Me, me, me and more me: Yoyo (Or Meme). The poor guy believed that with his egocentric attitude he earned a place in our hearts that only he was able to see, because the reality of things was that no one could stand his presence for a long time, since his attitude was so narcissistic that it seemed a cartoon. That first night I came to think that it was a prank by the more advanced students, a kind of hidden camera in which they had put an actor with an exaggerated degree of egocentrism in front of us so that we would discover a personality disorder on stage. But not. Yoyo was real and his exploits in the field of narcissism were already famous in those days. I once heard him speak with great admiration of a prestigious professor on campus and I was amazed by this change in his personality until he concluded his appreciation by saying: "He is almost as good as I will be in a few years." As you can imagine, there were very few people who wanted to be by his side and most of the few friends he had were new students who were fooled by his supposed genius until Yoyo's attitude bored them and they looked for new directions. All his friendships were fleeting and he knew it. His response to this phenomenon was to repeat that he didn't need anyone because he could take care of himself. College ended for me and my classmates and I lost track of him for several years until one fall morning I walked into a specialty bookstore in downtown Boston and was surprised to find him on the other side of the counter. I greeted him with surprise without being able to remember his name: "Hey…!" The awkward gap between my expression and my brain's fruitless search for his name ended when he said, "Yoyo, you can call me Yoyo if you want, that's how everyone knew me, right?" A little embarrassed at having shared the joke with my university colleagues, I had to accept that it was indeed the case. "Don't worry, Bill, years have passed since that and today I think I deserved that hateful nickname," he said with a gesture of acceptance on his shoulders. "After all, I was an unbearable guy who knew nothing about life," he added. He told me that if he had time he would like to have coffee with me after finishing his shift at the bookstore and I gladly accepted. The bug of curiosity had bitten me when I heard his critical words about the past. So we met in a cafe after he returned from work and he told me in broad strokes his story. When he finished university, he was still as lonely and conceited as before and believed that his character would help him make his way in professional life. Big mistake. One by one, the doors of the psychological clinics were closed because, as he said over his cup of coffee, "no one wanted a crazy narcissist treating patients when he was the one who needed to receive care." He then decided that the situation was probably due to his colleagues' envy of his "genius" and decided to establish his own practice. He rented a nice office in the city center, hired a secretary, and ran a risky marketing campaign in which he plastered city buses with his face. After a few days he began receiving patients. "You wouldn't believe it, Bill, they came in droves believing that the advertising guy could listen to all their problems and help them find a solution." But what they found was a guy who didn't listen to anyone and only wanted to talk about himself. It seemed like the height of a psychologist. "I wasn't a good professional, they paid me for their consultations in the hope of therapy and all they got were pedantic lectures from a guy who kept talking about how great he was," he told me. As the days went by, the magic of marketing disappeared and his practice emptied as quickly as it had filled. The bills were pressing and his name appeared stained in the union: no one wanted to hire him, much less associate with him to cover office expenses. After a few months he found himself in the painful situation of closing the office and assuming a heavy load of debts that destroyed his assets. Hitting rock bottom led him to absurdly take refuge in drink and after a "hell" of several years living in shelters and eating from charities, he felt that he had hit rock bottom and sought help from social services. "I understood the hard way that I was not the center of the world and that I could not pretend to be. There are millions of people and they are all worth the same as me, but I didn't know how to see that before going to therapy," he assured me with tears in his eyes. He had learned, he said, the value of empathy and humility. The importance of understanding that the ego can be our worst enemy. "Now I am working in this bookstore to pay my debts and return to the professional world, it is difficult because my name is still associated with Yoyo, the arrogant guy who is not able to see others."

Understanding the value of the people around you is essential to becoming a vitamin person. It's simple: think about how people who show no interest in you make you feel, even though the context in which they meet would imply a connection. This is a basic trait of a person that we would all like to have around, because it lays the foundational basis for healthy relationships: reciprocity. It's not about showing interest in others waiting for them to show it in you, it's about showing genuine interest and that's it. If you do not receive it back, you can close the door quietly, because you will be at peace with yourself for having acted under the correct premise.

How do I do it? I have a couple of recommendations.

Ask

The beginning of everything is to demonstrate that interest and that is achieved by asking. How are you? How is going your life? How are your projects progressing? The caliber of the questions will be limited by your relationship with people, you can't ask someone on public transport how their life is going, but perhaps if they are an older person you can ask them if they want to take your seat. Very easy. It's not about asking the awkward questions that annoying relative usually asks at a family dinner. Don't be indiscreet or nosy, show interest and learn to read others' willingness to tell or not keep things to themselves. Interest in others is also marked by knowing how to read their gestures. If their answers are evasive, do not insist, that is not interest, it is the beginning of harassment and you will only look like the annoying person who learned a questionnaire to feign interest.

Interest is love

My mother used to tell me that no one would wish me as much success in life as she does. Well, yes, my father. But outside the family nucleus it is difficult to find someone who can reach the same level. Even so, it is important to understand that interest is a way of expressing the love and affection we feel for people. If we believe that we love someone, we must know how to show it beyond physical affection. Knowing how a person is doing and how their dreams are progressing is a beautiful sign of affection. Make it.

The sweetest sound

This is a golden rule: learn the names of the people you meet and repeat them. Refer to them by name. The sweetest sound a human being can hear is his name. I don't know what you think, but I consider that expressions like "pretty" are devalued. In Spain it is used so frequently that it has lost its meaning and now any stranger calls a person handsome or pretty to charge them for a coffee. If you learn people's names, they will feel that you truly care about them and appreciate them like that Bill or Mary and not like a "hey."

Active listening

I already talked about this technique in the chapter dedicated to the need to listen to others, but I think it is important to reiterate it when it comes to demonstrating our interest in others. We all like to be listened to carefully and that the questions asked are related to what we say and are not a way of directing the conversation towards the interests of the other. Listen with interest if you are really interested in a person. You don't need to feign interest in people you're not interested in. It is logical that not all people on the planet are in our hearts.

The importance they deserve

All human beings want to feel that we matter. What's more, most people you talk to tend to feel superior to us for obvious reasons: they confuse self-esteem with ego. Beyond assessing whether this is good or bad, try to make it clear to them that you sincerely recognize their value and importance. It's not about lying, it's about recognizing and attributing value to the people around us. Many times we talk about the immense love we feel for a person, but our actions do not show it. Thus it is of little use to believe that we love.

Work your memory

A very simple way to show interest in others is to remember the things that are important to them. Dates, events or even your words. A friend used to start his sentences with a filler that earned him friends here and there. He told you: "It's just as you say, Bill…" and he quoted a phrase that you would have actually said in the past. You have to be really interested in someone to remember their words. Try it.

Read emotions

Sometimes we don't want to say how we feel. We carry a weight in our hearts but we remain silent because we do not want to bother others with our concerns and feelings. Well, we can be silent but our gestures will give us away. Learning to read these gestures is a powerful tool to show interest in others. If you know how to read faces and emotions, you will achieve a special connection with those around you. They will feel that you really care about them because even without mentioning it, you knew what they felt.

I am glad for your joy

If a person does not have positive feelings about their friends' success, they are not really your friend. If a person is frustrated because his environment achieves achievements, his heart does not harbor goodness. And that shows. A patient told me a few years ago that he had a dilemma: he didn't know if he should end his relationship with his best friend. They had known each other for many years and were great friends of deep conversations and beers. They once tried it romantically but it didn't work. That didn't change their friendship and they saw each other once a week to talk about their lives. However, he inherited some money and bought an apartment. When he told her the news, she looked upset and congratulated him briefly with a bitter expression on her face. He thought something was happening in her intimate life and asked her. Everything was in order and to allay her suspicions, he insisted on the topic of the apartment: she seemed upset and confused. When he told her he was eager to show it to her, she made up one excuse after another and he didn't insist. He came to the conclusion that she was jealous and not really happy about his happiness. My recommendation was: manage your affection. There are people who love us until we succeed. Our joy reminds them of their bitterness and they will try to drag us down with them. Don't be like that and if you are like that, stay away from anyone who causes these types of feelings in you. In the long run you will be the most affected.

Let's make life easy

The time we will spend alive is so short that I will waste no time explaining it. Therefore, if we find people to whom we can give our love and attention, we must make their lives easy. The principle of reciprocity says that they will make ours easier. If we are interested in a person, we can show it with small gestures such as managing our negative emotions, controlling resentment and frustration. There is no point in living this type of relationship of reproaches and bitterness: if you are really interested in the person, you have two options: make (and make) your life easy by controlling your emotions, or abandon the relationship for the good of both. If you are interested in a person, make their life easy: small favors, offer your help, explain what they don't know, spend time with them, share what you have. It's a way to be happy.

17 Expect nothing in return

The consumer society has made us believe that we must calculate what we will receive in exchange for what we give. It tells us that each of our actions is a transaction in which we make an exchange. I give and I receive. That is not always correct, since it conditions our relationships at a commercial level that prevents us from enjoying the fact of delivering. Just that: deliver. The basis of generosity is based on the ancient principle that giving is better than receiving. Breaking that can be dangerous for our harmony, as it will determine interested behavior that goes against the current of a vitamin person's energy.

The logic that we must receive something every time we give is a prison that limits our freedom of action. Every time we feel a spontaneous desire to perform an action regardless of what we can get from it, we will find ourselves inside the corset that prevents us from being ourselves.

I am not a religious guy, but we cannot deny the positive teachings in terms of human relations that some leaders have left us, such as Mother Teresa of Calcutta, known for her help to those most in need. "Always give the best, and the best will come," this woman had as a mantra and curiously, generosity can have this effect without us even looking for it. A study carried out by the University of Zurich established that generosity is also a source of happiness. In the research, published in the journal Nature Communications, it was established that participating volunteers were happier when they spent money on other people.

The team from the University of Zurich asked 50 people to think of a gift for a loved one. Then they were given money and the group was divided into two: some could spend the money on themselves and the others had to buy a gift. Magnetic resonance imaging showed that areas associated with happiness were activated more in those who bought the gift.

The study established that generous decisions and happiness were related to the interaction between two brain areas, the temporal-parietal junction and the central striatum. So, for us to feel good about generous acts, these regions involved in empathy and social cognition need to 'overwrite' selfish motives in areas related to rewards, as the newspaper La Vanguardia reported at the time.

But the research did not stop there: according to the study, the amount of money spent was not important in the psychological impact of the event, so this could indicate that small gestures towards our environment - such as giving your partner a massage - could have the same effect.

But this has not been the only work on the subject. In 2006, Jorge Moll, from the United States National Institute of Health, found that when people give charity, the regions of their brains associated with pleasure, social connection and trust are activated. Scientists also believe that altruistic behaviors produce the desired endorphins in the brain, generating feelings of satisfaction and happiness.

Stephen G. Post, professor of Preventive Medicine and Ph. D. – researcher and best-selling author who has dedicated much of his work to learning about the benefits of giving – has found that being generous brings health benefits because It reduces stress and thus prevents countless diseases, while reducing levels of anxiety and depression. According to their work, carried out with older adults who volunteer, doing this type of activity results in lower levels of stress, anxiety and depression.

Generosity is especially attractive to us when it arises from the very need of the person who offers. We tend to value receiving help from someone who needs it more, because it makes us feel their empathy towards us and their desire for us to be safe. That is why there is a kind of global consensus about the absurdity of wealth accumulation when a person has reached a certain threshold. Let's say 100 million euros. But prejudice leads us to the feeling that these types of people are the least willing to share their wealth with a sense of justice. We often see significant donations from billionaires to the State, however, these donations are only a fraction of the taxes they would have to pay if the legal headquarters of their companies were not located in tax havens. But that is another subject. I imagine that if you are reading this book, you do not belong to that minimum percentage of the world's population and what you are looking for is to become a better person, a person for whom your friends smile when they see you arrive.

In reality, generosity is an attitude of life, a philosophy from which we carry out our daily lives and does not apply only to money. Generosity exists in all areas of life and is much more noticeable when it occurs in the area of time. I can give away a hundred euros and earn it back in a few hours of work. But I will never get an hour of my life back. So when I give it to a noble cause, when I am generous with my time sharing with others, I am giving the most valuable thing I have. And even if I don't expect anything in return and my attitude arises from a noble gesture, I will always receive something in return. It can be an experience, a lesson, a learning or a memory. Every act of our lives involves receiving information, our brain is a scanner that never stops collecting data and the more diverse our field of action is, the more plasticity we will have, so why deny ourselves?

Let's see some ways to cultivate this gift:

Share something that means a lot to you
The first step in testing and cultivating generosity is what you share. If I have a lot of chocolates and I share a couple with my brother, I'm not exactly being generous. But if I share my beloved bicycle, I come closer to the true essence of this gift. Generosity means detachment and appreciation for the other, since we give them what we want most in the hope that they feel as happy as we feel with that thing. As I mentioned, it is not only about material objects, it can also be your knowledge or your time.

Cancel your small merchant
This is advice that would probably be banned in business school, but it is the basis of generosity. Don't expect anything in return for what you give. If you are a calculator, a person who believes that everything must be paid for, I have bad news for you. Not only are you not generous, but you will have a couple of disappointments along the way. Life is full of moments when giving without receiving is a gift in itself.

I also think it is important to remember that you should not expect them to use what you are selflessly giving away for what you want them to use it for.

You delivered something because you wanted to deliver it, up to that point you have control, the rest is not your concern and can be a source of frustration for both people. No one gives a gift with conditions, otherwise it is not a gift.

There are those who say that you should never remind people that you gave them something at some point. I do not agree with this statement, since generosity must also be applied to ourselves. If at any time we consider that we are immersed in a manipulative relationship that constantly asks us not to give, it seems quite healthy to suggest remembering everything we have given. There are people who give the best years of their lives to a partner and when they argue, they tell them that they have never given them anything. That is not the case and you should not confuse generosity with a lack of self-love. Of course, this does not mean that we should keep a logbook of our good deeds.

The gift

I like to think of generosity as a gift. That is why not everyone owns it and is so appreciated and valued. When I think about it this way, I want it strongly: I want that blessing too. I also want to have the ability to build bonds of affection from detachment. Generosity makes us people closer to what we think when we evoke the concept of humanity.

Accept the generosity of another

Throughout my life I have encountered very generous people who feel uncomfortable when others are generous to them. They are the first when it comes to giving and do not skimp on sharing what they have, even if it is little, so that other people feel comfortable. However, when it is their turn to be on the other side of the counter, they become uncomfortable and refuse to receive what is offered to them, as if in some mysterious way they feel that they do not deserve it and that their role in life is different. Don't fall into that trap. Your role in life is to be happy and sometimes receiving is part of that happiness. Furthermore, generosity often has a knock-on effect, because when a person feels blessed by another person's generosity, they become sensitive and prone to having the same effect on other people. Don't cut the chain, let others be generous to you.

The limits of generosity

In a cafe in London I found a small painting with a phrase that stuck in my memory: "If you are one of those who give, you must know your limits because those who take never have limits." It seems important to me to emphasize the importance of knowing how to set certain limits, but this applies to everything: my mother already said it, not so much that it burns the saint nor so little that it does not illuminate him. Everything in excess becomes harmful and what you have to control in this case is not the goodness of your heart but relationships that are not balanced. Because someone who gives without expecting anything in return is pure of heart, he is a noble and good being that everyone wants by their side, but he who becomes a resource for other people who abuse that generosity is sadly complicit in his tragedy. . Because not having balanced relationships is undoubtedly a tragedy that we cannot ignore.

Live generosity without restraints, but do not allow it to become a form of abuse. Remember, those who take, those who take, those who abuse do not know limits and at that moment you have to act.

I once met a person with some fame in the entertainment world. She was simply charming. A lot of charisma and her words were so precise and loquacious, so lucid and funny, that you wanted to share all your time with her. After a few months we began a loving relationship that initially filled me with joy. After a few weeks I understood why this person was single. When I arrived at his house, he greeted me with his beautiful smile and some jokes before going on to tell me a series of very interesting things that had happened to him. I was talking about the great faces of the show with enthusiasm and after a couple of hours I hadn't found the moment - I would never find it, of course - to ask myself how my day had been. In the short time we shared, I did a lot for her. I did it, of course, selflessly and with joy: his joy in the path his career was taking was enough for me. But, after a while, those eternal nights of talking about herself and her world ended up boring me: I exist too, I told myself. When I told him my feelings, his reaction confirmed the imbalance in our relationship: "I'm sorry Bill, I never would have imagined that you would want to talk about your life too." Don't let something like this happen to you. Don't be the other side either: they don't go far in the long run. Giving without receiving is very pleasant, but it is also pleasant to receive without having asked for it.

Self-esteem plays a fundamental role in this limit, since it is important that you know what you deserve. All human beings deserve the same, but not all of us are fully aware of this. Many people are willing to settle for little in order not to be alone or sadly have been victims of psychological abuse that has made them believe that they do not deserve the same as they give. It is not like this. Remember it every day. If necessary, write it on a piece of paper and stick it in a visible place: you are worth a lot and you deserve everything. This type of unequal relationships can occur in all areas: a loved family member, your partner, your friends or even with your co-workers.

18 Look with the eyes of a child

The British writer Aldous Huxley, author of the masterpiece Brave New World, used to say that the secret of genius is to preserve the child's spirit into old age, which means never losing enthusiasm. Have you noticed the eyes of a child when faced with such everyday phenomena as lightning? Do you remember what you felt when you were a child and they proposed an adventure that you had never experienced, like climbing a mountain? Enthusiasm is the ability to continue seeing things as if it were the first time and in that children have a great advantage. Their newness on earth allows them to marvel at everything, every day is magical and knowledge is a kind of sacred revelation that drives them crazy.

I have good news for you: being a child can last a lifetime. Seeing the world through the eyes of a child is an option available to the mind and requires some work, but it is possible and it will help you be a magnetic person because, in the world we live in, those who are capable of thinking outside the box , if they have authentic logic, they stand out. I would like you to remember a little about some of the things you thought when you were a child. Many of our childhood ideas had a logic that escaped the twisted logic of the world and somehow made much more sense than the order of our society makes. I remember my little son Mike one afternoon watching the news on the television. They were passing a report about a terrorist attack in

Israel. The author had used a bomb to end the lives of some innocent beings and my son, very distressed because he has always been a very sweet and sensitive being, told me almost through tears: "Dad, but why don't they close the store where Do they sell those bombs? "That way no one could buy them and harm others." His reflection touched my heart and I did not have the courage to explain to him how the matter worked. Another day I heard him ask his mother: "If God made Adam out of clay, does it fall apart when it rains?" There are some reflections that can be of a furious anarchic nature, even questioning the foundations of our society. One of those was the son of a colleague who asked him why, if God loved men so much, he created hurricanes that destroyed their houses.

The process of growing up involves detaching yourself from that pure and natural logic to learn one that coincides with that of our society. Curiously, this new logic is increasingly similar around the world to the globalization process. Just a few decades ago, a child in South America might have grown up with a very different worldview than their peers in the United States, to say the least. Today, the unique discourse of Western societies has led us to believe that there is only one possible society. But that is another topic. The truth is that growing up and abandoning that natural logic of children is an inevitable process: institutions mold us to be more similar every day and we talk about "learning" to describe a molding process like in a mass factory that , among other things, wants to take away from us such powerful blessings as the capacity for wonder. Nowadays it is no surprise to anyone that you can talk in real time with a person who is thousands of kilometers away, that you can even see them on a small screen. We take for granted such wonderful facts as that humanity has been able to create devices that take off from the earth and travel projected through the air at a speed of a thousand kilometers per hour, covering in a short time distances that only a century ago were impossible. We have become accustomed to magic and that is why it has been losing its shine.

However, there are people who still retain that capacity for wonder. People who are able to see the world with fresh eyes, as if they had grown only in body and their eyes were still as pure as when they were eight years old. These are magical people who help us see everyday life in a special way, who seem to have fun with what some call work and find room for laughter despite the great drama of existence. Think for a moment about your environment, about the people around you and that you appreciate. I am sure that you will be able to identify some of these characteristics in some and it is very likely that these are the people you are most attracted to. It's because they know how to appreciate the simplicity of things. And in simplicity there is truth, beauty and joy. A cliché often suggests that the most valuable things in life are free. Well, I agree with a small point: it's not that they are free, we pay for them over time, something much more valuable than money.

I would like to return to Huxley's concept of enthusiasm with which I began this chapter to associate it with something fundamental in life: passion. We must learn from children the passion for things because it will make us live each day with intensity. I understand that not all people are fortunate enough to work on something they are passionate about. Sometimes economic needs lead us to mortgage our dreams for a time, to park them on the side of the road while we organize our lives. You must keep in mind that time is unforgiving and that parking is very expensive. You shouldn't spend too much time there or the bill will be terrible: reaching the sad moment of impossible questions like "what if I had cheered up?" It is an irremediable tragedy. That is why we must pursue our passion with enthusiasm. When I was young I liked to subscribe to the trend of those who call this "being hungry." Hunger is a driving force. Here I am referring to physical hunger, the need for food, and the hunger for success. I don't want to say hunger for money, because that is a concept of triumph that is very far from true happiness. Money helps us, without a doubt, but it is not the guarantee of happiness. Only the satisfaction of doing what we are passionate about will give us true success. And for that we have to live with enthusiasm and carry the hope that we will be able to achieve what we dream of. Just like when we were kids.

Divergent thinking

One of the ways that modern psychology calls a child's curious look is Divergent thinking or lateral thinking. It is about creative ways of looking at a topic and finding alternative solutions to the problems that we face every day. It is something that a child would look for at all costs when asked a logical question. He knows that the traditional way to climb a building is to take the stairs or the elevator, but in his creative mindset he could propose a springboard. Divergent thinking is precisely that: seeing new ways of thinking that question existing ones and are more effective. Because although the trampoline will be more fun, it may not be the most practical.

It is a type of intelligence linked to creativity that constantly questions the pre-established to find new paths, hence its name, since we are talking about ideas that "diverge" from the traditional way.

People who use divergent thinking are spontaneous since their inner being is inviting them to propose new routes. A person who does not think this way simply accepts what they have been given as a solution and does not question what is established.

These are also people with an open mind to whom nothing will seem completely "far-fetched", because this is how humanity has achieved many of its great discoveries. Remember the case of Christopher Columbus and his arrival to the American continent. The guy believed in something that no one else believed in his time: that the earth was round, and not flat, and that through there he could reach the East Indies and bypass the Ottoman blockade to bring species to the European continent. And he achieve it. Nicolás Copernicus also achieved this by ensuring that the Earth revolved around the sun and not the sun around the Earth, as was believed at the time. There are thousands of cases of divergent thinking in which openness to new ideas, to ideas that challenged the established, led to wonderful discoveries.

People with this type of thinking have a great imagination (like children!) and visualize completely original ideas. That's why we're talking about very creative people who propose several answers to the same question.

As you can imagine, they are very curious people and constantly take risks. It is not for nothing that some of them were considered heretics or crazy for defending ideas that in their time were considered absurd.

One of the advantages of people who see the world with divergent thinking is that they do not remain stuck in their beliefs. What's more, they tend to constantly challenge them, because they know that what we take for granted today may be a big mistake.

On the other hand, one of the disadvantages of divergent thinking is that the multiplicity of answers to a question can make a person digress and be impractical when it comes to solving a specific problem. Sometimes their solutions can be very creative but not very useful.

Imagination

People who keep in their hearts a child capable of looking at the world with surprise have a great imagination. That is why they are usually behind great inventions and discoveries: they do not accept the world as such, they like to see new things in it and they go around the world with completely original ideas. The ability to imagine a different world has a very powerful effect on those around them, as it is a way of challenging what is established and building personal universes. Imagination allows them to see that the world is not just black or white, that there is a wide range of colors and that reality is a perception that we can change. If you want to stimulate your imagination, I recommend that you do the same thing you do when you want to run a marathon: train. Give your brain space to imagine. Disconnect a little from the given world and try to create new universes. I suggest that you use the time you spend aimlessly browsing social networks to develop new ideas on a given topic. For example, imagine what the planet will be like in a hundred years. Don't let fiction influence you, try to create scenarios independent of all the ones we already know in film and television. It's just an exercise of imagination, anything can help. You can take a walk, walking is a good stimulus for the imagination.

How to stimulate divergent thinking and the child's gaze?

We often hear the expression that you have to think outside the box. But which box? Most human beings believe that it is others who live immersed in a bubble. Few of us are willing to accept that we are inside. It is something similar to what happens when we talk about "the people." We usually use this term to refer to everyone else and blame "the people" for certain customs, as if we were a third, abstract person in society. Well, the first step to entering a disruptive way of thinking is to accept that we are inside a bubble and that our environment probably makes us believe that everything we think is correct because they think in a similar way. This is known as the echo chamber or resonance box. It basically means that people associate with other people who think relatively the same as us. This is why we usually get big surprises with the results of the elections. This is what happened in 2016 when Donald Trump became president of the United States. You could hear hundreds of people saying that they couldn't believe this was true: "me and all my friends voted for Hilary." Sure, the world you live in looks like your desires, but that doesn't mean it's the majority. So we must accept that we are inside a bubble and the best way to know this is to analyze our own bubble. What are the beliefs that I share with those around me? What kinds of ideas would be despised by me and those around me? Am I willing to listen to ideas that question everything I think? It's about seeing life from different perspectives and not being tied to any one.

I'm going to tell you a story: at the beginning of the 20th century, malaria was an epidemic that seriously threatened the development of societies in the tropics of the planet. It took hundreds of thousands of lives a year - it still does - and seemed out of control without scientists knowing what to do. Among the community of scholars, it began to be suspected that this disease was transmitted by some animal. But for which one? Well, everything led them to believe that the culprit of the evil was the cockroach, so small containers with water were installed at the legs of the beds to prevent these insects from climbing there while people slept. Serious error: the true person responsible for transmitting the disease is the Anopheles mosquito and the containers with water left by the doctors were an excellent breeding ground for its larvae, which further enhanced the growth of the disease. The beliefs we have can be wrong and, worse still, can be extremely harmful, so we must be willing to question them if we want to live "outside the box."

I'm going to give you some practical tips to cultivate divergent thinking.

Keep a notebook of ideas

Scientific studies have established that human beings have about 60,000 thoughts a day, many of them composed of new ideas. We tend to believe that if it is a great idea, we will remember it forever, after all it is something very new and powerful. Serious mistake: our brain does not retain everything we think and to prevent our genius from being lost in the darkness of oblivion, it is quite practical to have a notebook where we write down what we think. Furthermore, it is proven that writing things down helps us memorize them and generate new ideas about this "seed." I recommend that you always carry a notebook with you.

The wonderful day to day

Don't you think it's incredible that just by turning a key, water appears from a faucet? Hot water? We are accustomed to events that a few years ago would have been unthinkable; if we lose the ability to be dazzled by them, we lose the ability to dream of new events. I invite you to live day to day from amazement. Let yourself be surprised by the simplicity and you will see how new ideas flow to you. Sometimes the best ideas are the simplest, give them a chance.

free expression

Take a sheet of paper and a pencil. If you have a set of colored pencils, so much the better. There are no rules. There are no rules and I only ask that you express yourself however you want. You can draw, you can write. Free writing and drawing are one of the best ways to channel thought. Let everything flow, don't think about your thoughts, let them out. If you practice free expression, over time you will see that there is much more inside you than you thought. Some writers use this technique to combat blank page syndrome. When they think they have nothing to write or that they are going through a block, they simply get in front of the keyboard and write whatever comes to mind. After a while they have "warmed up" and feel ready to write about the topic they had thought about.

Brainstorm

Think of a problem. Now think about the solutions. Yes, plural. Solutions. Write down all the answers on a sheet of paper. As you strive to find new solutions, you will realize that there were many more options than you initially thought. This makes me think of the story of a teacher who asked his students how to measure the height of a building with a barometer. The expected answer had to do with air pressure, but one of them said he could tie the barometer to a rope and throw it from the roof, then measure the rope. The same student said he could grab the barometer and measure its length and the length of his shadow, then measure the length of the building's shadow and apply a ratio calculation. He also said that you could hold the barometer against the wall of the building and mark how many times the device could fit as you went up, then count the times and multiply them by its size. They are all correct methods!

End the fear

The brake for many people in different areas of their lives is fear: what people will say, the fear of failure, the fear of standing out from others and being noticed. This is one of the enemies of divergent thinking and childish logic. If you live thinking about what others will say about you, it is very likely that you walk in the shadows, that you prefer to stay with what has been thought and established and that you accept the ideas of others as your own because that way no one will ask you anything. . That's a very respectable way to exist, but I don't think you'll stand out much. The fear of risk leaves us where we are. Whether or not this is worth it is something that each person must judge. However, I believe that if you aspire to become a better version of yourself, the vitamin person, this will relegate you to a simple painkiller.

Child spirit

Well, let's return to the idea of childlike thinking with simple ways of living life under the impulse of enthusiasm. After all, that's what we've come for. Living is a miracle and every day can be a party if you decide so. You must have already heard that the best way to not work a single day in your life is to choose a job that you enjoy. Since this sounds like a utopian fantasy that not all of us can afford, we can also reconfigure our vision of the work we have to find fun in it.

I will give you simple advice from my inner child.

-Smile and enjoy the simple things. Don't get angry easily, enjoy the absurd. If you mistakenly put sugar instead of salt, give it a try and explore. Remember that tradition is just the illusion of eternity.

-Don't be hard on the mistakes of others. We can all make mistakes. If there is no bad intention, look for empathy in your heart and treat other people's mistakes as a small lesson.

-And where is the smile? Try to repeat this question to yourself throughout the day. I know that not all of us can smile constantly, but try. Imitate the children and you will see that joy will flow.

-You want to be my friend? Think for a second: how long has it been since you made a new friend?

-Good morning. Saying hello is not bad, it establishes connections with strangers and softens the smile. It will give you some serotonin.

-Sing and dance. What does it matter if you don't know how to do it, try to live life like a party. Sing and dance, you will see that your disposition to joy becomes reality.

-Play. You are the character of your own video game, the tasks you have to do are the different tests that you have to pass to advance to the next stage.

Look at things with humor, after all you have to do them, so it's better if you do it with a good face and a happy soul.

-The power of simplicity. Did you see that that cloud looks like a rabbit coming out of a magician's hat? Did you notice that pigeons eat things that we don't see? The essential is invisible to the eye, Antoine de Saint-Exupéry, author of The Little Prince, once said.

Childish look does not mean immaturity

I would like to close this chapter by making a brief comment about the big difference between having the enthusiasm of a child and the indolent attitude of someone who is immature. Looking into the eyes with a childlike soul has nothing to do with letting go of our responsibilities. It is curious and sad the drift that the word child has taken in our language. We use it as if it were a negative characteristic that denotes naivety. Is naivety a bad thing? The purity of one's gaze can be a great gift that I think is appropriate to preserve. A professional magician once said that he would never like to live in a society in which no one could deceive, because this would mean that we would find ourselves in a society in which no one trusts. People who are victims of deception are often blamed for being naive, this seems like a mistake to me: the culprit is the one who deceived them, not the one who trusted them in good faith, as children do.

The child's look implies wonder and joy, it implies enthusiasm and emotion. Immaturity, on the other hand, is closely linked to a lack of empathy with other people because the ego does not let these people see a little beyond their noses. This is something a child would never do. Immature people do not know how to see their responsibilities and act as if someone else was going to take charge of their lives. That's not what we're looking for. The desired attitude is a mixture of a virgin spirit with a commitment to oneself without losing track of others. If we are immature and do not have empathy, it is very unlikely that we will have divergent thinking, since immaturity implies believing that our vision of the world is the only valid one.

If you think that acting irrationally is living life like a child, I think you have a problem. Only someone who is immature would be able to avoid introspection because they are not interested in learning from their mistakes. A child, on the other hand, is very interested in learning from his mistakes and from others.

19 Letter to my son

I would like to close this book with a personal license. After all, the lessons I have presented here are part of my reflections and have been driven by a very special figure: my son John. Each of the words written here has been thought with the affection of a father to a son, as a way of leaving a record of everything I would like to teach my son and, if possible, my son's children. There is no literary pretension in it, just the love of a father.

Chicago, June 2022

Dear John,

Beloved son. I have decided to write these lines because I would like what I want to tell you to be recorded here with the power of writing. I know very well that our communication is excellent, but there are things that I think are better to express in writing. I've always thought of letters as a record of time. When I am not by your side physically you can make me revive just by reading this text. Although we both know that I will be by your side, within you, with every word and teaching.

I want you to be happy. I wouldn't say very happy or the happiest. Happiness is a unique, pure state. There are no nuances in it, You are happy because you are, without further ado. Happiness is not a goal either: some mistakenly believe that they should aim for happiness as if it were a destination they must reach. I wonder, and when they get there, what? Aren't goals something fragile and temporary?

I want you to be happy when you get up in the morning and stay happy until night, to be happy in your dreams and in your future.

To help you be happy I only have words to offer you. They have been written with all the love my heart can contain. I hope you take them as that: instructions from someone who loves you dearly and wants the best for you.

I don't know if you have heard that "vitamin person", and if not, I will help you: they are the people that we all want to have by our side because they make us shine and only generate good feelings in us. I would like you to be one of them. May every person around you feel that you are indispensable in their life.

I give you this book, in it you will find the words that I would like to remind you of every time you forget them. You, and all human beings, have the ability to become an engine of change in our environment, a flame in the darkness for those who have lost their way. Read them calmly and consistently. I would like to tell you that there is no rush, but there is no rush. Time flies and the best time to begin a path of construction, goodness, healthy spirituality and education in goodness was yesterday. The second best time is today.

Please don't give up. Throughout your life you will find traps and false joys. Don't be dazzled by crystals and beads that only shine without any value. Everything that is truly worthwhile costs. Do your best to make every day a holiday full of love and achievements. Don't leave for tomorrow what you can do today, even less so if it involves building yourself as a good person.

I will be by your side, to the extent possible and until the natural course of things allows us.

Love, Bill. Your father.

ABOUT THE AUTHOR

Bill Waits is a prestigious American psychologist, currently one of the greatest exponents of behavioral psychology. In the past, Waits published the book Unforced Errors, where he talks about the importance of mistakes as a starting point for learning. On this occasion, Professor Waits takes the concept of the "vitamin person" as a forced foot to establish a guide on how to be a good person and be happy. This is an approach to his work as a therapist in which he tries to expose his patients to the most common mistakes of humanity to avoid wasting time in this race that is life. .